D1484049

CREATION
of the
MODERN MIDDLE EAST

The Palestinian National Authority

CREATION

of the

MODERN MIDDLE EAST

CREATION
of the
MODERN MIDDLE EAST

The Palestinian National Authority

Second Edition

John G. Hall | Series Editor: Arthur Goldschmidt Jr.

Additional text by Adam Woog

CHELSEA HOUSE
PUBLISHERS
An imprint of Infobase Publishing

The Palestinian National Authority

Copyright © 2009 by Infobase Publishing

Chelsea House
An imprint of Infobase Publishing
132 West 31st Street
New York NY 10001

Library of Congress Cataloging-in-Publication Data
Hall, John G., 1950-
 The Palestinian National Authority / by John G. Hall ; additional text by Adam Woog. — 2nd ed.
     p. cm. — (Creation of the modern Middle East)
 Includes bibliographical references and index.
 ISBN 978-1-60413-020-1 (hardcover)
 1. Palestine—History—19th century—Juvenile literature. 2. Palestine—History—20th century—Juvenile literature. 3. Jews—Palestine—History—19th century—Juvenile literature. 4. Jews—Palestine—History—20th century—Juvenile literature. 5. Palestinian National Authority—Juvenile literature. [1. Arab-Israeli conflict—Juvenile literature.] I. Woog, Adam, 1953- II. Title. III. Series.
 DS125.H28 2008 956.94—dc21

Series design by Annie O'Donnell
Cover design by Jooyoung An

Printed in the United States of America

Bang EJB 10 9 8 7 6 5 4 3 2 1

This book is printed on acid-free paper.

Contents

Palestine and the Palestinians

Anyone who pays any attention to the news cannot miss hearing about issues in the Middle East. Stories of the conflicts there appear in local newspapers in the United States, on the evening news, and even in short news clips on MTV. The issues are covered extensively in national news magazines such as *Time* and *Newsweek*, and they also show up in pop culture and entertainment magazines such as *People*. Images and headlines of the "Crisis in the Middle East," particularly of the conflict between the Palestinians and the Israelis, are everywhere.

Almost any newspaper or magazine, or any morning or evening news broadcast, will have a sampling of headlines like these:

Announcement of U.S. Peace Trip Followed by Deadly Clashes
Deadly Day of Conflict
Terror Attacks Kill 14 Israelis
Hamas Hails "Liberation" of Gaza

Middle East news pierces through even the biggest news stories elsewhere, competing for front-page coverage with other stories of natural disasters, conflicts, wars, and other newsworthy events. This is especially true for news of the conflicts between Israeli Jews and Palestinian Arabs.

For the past 60 years, the conflict between these two groups has demanded constant media attention, not just in the United States, but also throughout the world. Still, despite the coverage, the topic remains complicated and difficult for many to understand. The constant media attention and the saturation of people's minds with images and headlines do not mean that people are any closer to understanding the "real" stories, the "real" sacrifices, and the tragic loss of human lives that have become part of the permanent landscape in this region.

THE LAND

Many scholars and historians trace the source of this conflict to 1948. That was the year the state of Israel was founded. This occasion immediately was marked by a war between the Arabs in the Middle East and the new state of Israel. Judging from these circumstances, it would seem that the scholars and historians are right: The founding of the state of Israel triggered the conflict between the Arabs and the Jews that has lasted for the past 60 years. On some level, that observation would be accurate, especially when considering all the supporting information. On the other hand, however, this explanation, regardless of its accuracy, doesn't tell the entire story. The images and headlines that erupt out of the Middle East on an almost daily basis have a much longer history that began in ancient times, more than 3,000 years ago. As a result, to fully appreciate the nature of the conflict, it

---

(opposite) The area of Palestine features a variety of terrain, including mountain ranges. These borders, however, have been moved to make room for Israel, causing conflict and war throughout the region. While the battle for the holiest of lands in modern times centers around ownership of Jerusalem and the West Bank, Palestine's historical territory once connected Africa, Europe, and Asia.

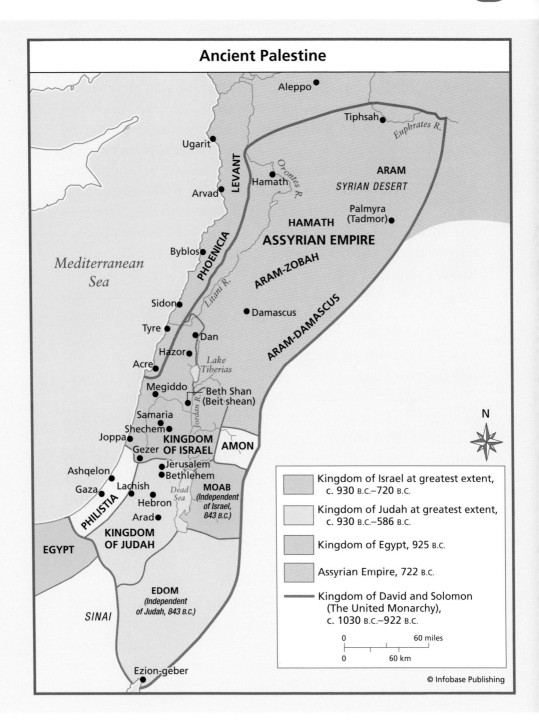

Ancient Palestine

Aleppo

Tiphsah

Euphrates R.

Ugarit

ARAM
SYRIAN DESERT

LEVANT

Hamath

Orontes R.

Arvad

Palmyra
(Tadmor)

HAMATH

ASSYRIAN EMPIRE

PHOENICIA

Byblos

Mediterranean
Sea

ARAM-ZOBAH

Litani R.

Sidon

Damascus

ARAM-DAMASCUS

Tyre

Dan

Hazor

Acre

Lake
Tiberias

Megiddo

Beth Shan
(Beit shean)

Jordan R.

Samaria

Shechem

Joppa

KINGDOM
OF ISRAEL

AMON

Gezer

Jerusalem

Ashqelon

Bethlehem

Gaza

Lachish

Dead
Sea

MOAB
(Independent
of Israel,
843 B.C.)

PHILISTIA

Hebron

Arad

KINGDOM
OF JUDAH

EGYPT

N

EDOM
(Independent
of Judah, 843 B.C.)

SINAI

Ezion-geber

Kingdom of Israel at greatest extent,
c. 930 B.C.–720 B.C.

Kingdom of Judah at greatest extent,
c. 930 B.C.–586 B.C.

Kingdom of Egypt, 925 B.C.

Assyrian Empire, 722 B.C.

Kingdom of David and Solomon
(The United Monarchy),
c. 1030 B.C.–922 B.C.

0   60 miles

0   60 km

© Infobase Publishing

would be beneficial to explore the history of Palestine and the people who have inhabited the land since ancient times.

The historic region known as Palestine covers a total area of about 10,435 square miles. It is about the size of Vermont, one of the smallest states in the United States. The region has an extremely diverse terrain and, generally speaking, may be divided into four parallel zones. First is a coastal plain running from west to east, consisting of fertile land with an abundance of underground water and plentiful rainfall. These plains have always been highly developed and planted with large stretches of citrus groves. Next is the hill region, predominantly rock but suitable for growing non-evergreen trees. Olives are this region's principal crop. In the winter, large acres of land are planted with wheat and barley. In the summer, corn, tomatoes, and other vegetables are grown using special cultivation techniques developed for dry regions. Then, there is the Jordan Valley region, which lies below sea level. The soil there is suitable for most kinds of cultivation, especially citrus and tropical fruits. Rainfall is usually too light, though, so farmers depend on irrigation from streams or from water that is pumped from the Jordan River. Finally, the Southern Desert or Negev region makes up nearly half the land of Palestine. The northern section consists of rich soil and is suitable for agriculture with the help of irrigation. The southern part consists of deeply eroded uplands and rift valleys.

THE PEOPLE

The word *Palestine* comes from *Philistia*, the name given by Greek writers to the land of the Philistines. In the twelfth century B.C., the Philistines occupied a small stretch of land on the southern coast among what are now Tel Aviv, Yafo, and Gaza. The Romans revived the name for this region in the second century A.D., when they referred to the area as *Syria Palaestina*.

The earliest known inhabitants of Palestine were the Canaanites. During the third millennium B.C., they lived in city-states, the most notable of which was Jericho. They developed an alphabet, and their religion was a major influence on the beliefs and practices of Judaism, Christianity, and Islam. Palestine's location at the center of routes linking three continents made it the meeting place for religious and cultural influences from Egypt, Syria, Mesopotamia, and Asia Minor. It also was the natural battleground for the great powers of the region and was subject to domination by adjacent empires, beginning with Egypt in the third millennium B.C.

After Egypt had conquered the Canaanites, Egyptian control and domination of the region was constantly challenged by an ethnically diverse group of invaders. These invaders, however, were defeated by the Egyptians and were absorbed by the Canaanites. Gradually, as Egyptian influence declined, new invaders appeared. One group was the Philistines, who had cultivated a highly civilized society on the coast of the Mediterranean Sea to the southeast of Judea, a part of what is now the West Bank. According to the Old Testament (Amos 9:7, Jeremiah 47:4, and Deuteronomy 2:23), they came from Caphtor, which modern scholars identify as Crete.

Most notable among the invaders, however, were the Hebrews, whose name means "those who pass from place to place." The Hebrews were a group of Semitic tribes that, according to tradition, migrated from Mesopotamia to Palestine during the second millennium B.C. Some scholars, however, trace Hebrew origin to "the wilderness," or the Sinai Peninsula, rather than to Mesopotamia.

Hebrew tribes probably immigrated to the region centuries before Moses led his people out of slavery in Egypt in about 1270 B.C. According to tradition, the Hebrews (also called the Twelve Tribes of Israel) finally defeated the Canaanites in about 1125 B.C., but they found the struggle with the Philistines more difficult. The Philistines' independent state on the southern coast of Palestine controlled a number of towns to the north and east. Superior in military organization, and using iron weapons, they severely defeated the Hebrews in about 1050 B.C. The Philistine

Palestine has always been coveted land, and the Philistines and Hebrews were constantly fighting for control of the area *(above)*. The famous Biblical story of the little Hebrew hero, David, against the Philistine giant, Goliath, is an example of one of the many battles between the two groups.

threat forced the Hebrews to unite and to establish a monarchy: Saul was the first king of ancient Israel, but it was David who finally defeated the Philistines shortly after 1000 B.C.

The unity of Israel and the gradual decline of other empires enabled David to establish a large independent state, with its capital at Jerusalem. After David's death, his son Solomon was the next great king of Israel. During Solomon's reign, the region enjoyed peace and prosperity, but after his death in 922 B.C. the kingdom was divided into Israel in the north and Judah in the south. The divided Israelites could no longer maintain their independence. Israel fell to Assyria in 722 and 721 B.C., and Judah was conquered by Babylonia in 586 B.C. As a result of this conquest, Jerusalem was destroyed and the Jews were exiled.

When Cyrus the Great of Persia conquered Babylonia in 539 B.C. he permitted the Jews to return to Judea (also spelled *Judah*), a district of Palestine. Under Persian rule the Jews were allowed considerable autonomy: They rebuilt their temple and the walls of Jerusalem. They also codified the Mosaic law, the Torah, which became the code of social life and religious observance.

Persian domination of Palestine was replaced by Greek rule when Alexander the Great of Macedonia conquered the region in 333 B.C. Alexander's successors, the Ptolemies of Egypt and the Seleucids of Syria, later ruled the country. The Seleucids tried to impose Greek culture and religion on the population, leading to a series of revolts by the Jewish inhabitants. The Maccabees revolted and set up an independent state, which lasted about 80 years, until Pompey the Great conquered Palestine for Rome and made it a province ruled by Jewish kings. It was during the rule of King Herod the Great (37–4 B.C.) that Jesus was born.

Two more Jewish revolts were suppressed in the following years. After the second revolt, numerous Jews were killed and many of the survivors were sold into slavery. It was during this time that Judea was renamed Syria Palaestina.

Palestine received special attention when Rome's Emperor Constantine made Christianity the official religion of the Roman Empire in A.D. 313. His mother, Helena, visited Jerusalem and Palestine, and from that time on, the region was looked upon as the Holy Land and became the focus of Christian pilgrimage. A golden age of prosperity, security, and culture followed. Most of the population assimilated to Greek and Christian traditions. Roman rule then was interrupted by a brief Persian occupation of Palestine from 614 to 629, and the rule was ended altogether when Muslim Arabs invaded Palestine and captured Jerusalem in A.D. 638.

This Arab conquest began 1,300 years of Muslim occupation. Palestine is holy to Muslims because, according to tradition, the Prophet Muhammad designated Jerusalem as the first *gibla*—the direction Muslims face when praying—and because Moses is believed to have ascended to heaven on a miraculous night journey from the area of Solomon's temple, where the Dome of the Rock was later built. After Mecca and Medina, Jerusalem is the third holiest city of the Islamic faith.

The Muslim rulers did not force their religion on the Palestinians, and more than three centuries passed before the majority converted to Islam. The majority of Palestinians also adopted Arabic language and culture. The remaining Christians and Jews were considered "People of the Book." They were allowed to govern their own communities and were permitted freedom of worship.

Palestine benefited from its religious importance to Islam during the period known as the Umayyad dynasty. It also benefited from the powerful Muslim Empire's trade and shared in the glory of Muslim civilization, especially when the Islamic world enjoyed a golden age in science, art, philosophy, and literature. Muslims preserved Greek learning and broke new ground in several fields, all of which later contributed to the Renaissance in Europe.

But when power shifted to Baghdad after new Muslim rulers took over in A.D. 750, Palestine fell into neglect. It suffered unrest and successive domination by Seljuks, Fatimids, and European crusaders, and, like the rest of the empire, Palestine gradually declined under Mamluk rule.

The Ottoman Empire defeated the Mamluks in 1517 and, with few interruptions, ruled Palestine until the winter of 1918. Under the Ottomans, the country was divided into several districts, such as that of Jerusalem. The administration of the districts was largely left to the responsibility of the Palestinian

Arabs, although the Christian and Jewish communities were granted a large degree of freedom. Palestine shared in the glory of the Ottoman Empire during the sixteenth century but declined when the empire started to weaken in the seventeenth century. The decline of Palestine in trade, agriculture, and population continued until the nineteenth century.

2

Palestine in the Nineteenth Century

The modern history of Palestine begins around the dawn of the nineteenth century and ends in 1948. For Palestinians, this period is known as the time before *al-Nakbah*, or "the catastrophic destruction of Palestine." These years can be divided into two main historical periods: The first covers the nineteenth century and the twentieth century up until World War I. The second begins, after World War I, with the establishment of the British Mandate of Palestine under the authority of the League of Nations.

During the 148 years before the creation of Israel, additional events occurred that were destined to have a profound impact on Palestine and the Palestinian Arabs who lived there. Foremost among these was the expansion of the British Empire. During the late nineteenth century, Great Britain was the dominant economic and political power in the world. As a result, it faced little competition from the other European powers. Left unchallenged, it succeeded in extending its power through informal influence without necessarily asserting formal political control. This would have increased the costs of government and entailed other responsibilities. The push for informal influence became known as the "imperialism of free trade."

The British did not establish many formal colonies, but they controlled other countries and peoples in order to have sources of raw materials and markets for their manufactured goods. In the Middle East, for example, the British wished to maintain the political stability of the region and, if possible, to prolong the sovereignty of the Ottoman Empire, in order to ensure the safety of the routes to India across Ottoman lands. They attempted for most of the nineteenth century to remain on friendly terms with the Ottomans in order to block their European rivals' ambitions, most notably Russia, and to keep open their lines of communication to the east. In the long run, this policy of "European intervention" transformed the social, economic, political, and cultural structure of Palestine, with devastating consequences for the indigenous Arab population of the country, as will be discussed in later chapters in this book.

Another historical event that had lasting consequences for the Palestinians was the rise of nationalism among the peoples of Central and Eastern Europe, which led to the intensification of anti-Semitism during the latter half of the nineteenth century. This in turn led to increased Jewish immigration to Palestine and the birth of the World Zionist Organization, which was created to solve Europe's "Jewish problem." These factors set in motion many of the antagonisms that have lasted until the present day and that have continued to shape attitudes and events in the Middle East, Israel, and the occupied territories of the West Bank and Gaza Strip, as well as among Palestinians in exile.

SHIFTING RELATIONSHIPS AMONG THE "PEOPLE OF THE BOOK"

European intervention in Palestine encouraged the process of European settlement in the country, transformed the economy, created new social classes, and rearranged power relationships among existing social groups, including recent Jewish settlers. For example, as will be discussed here later on, European powers helped the Ottoman Empire fight Russia during the Crimean War (1853–1856). Afterwards, the Ottoman government issued a decree granting Christians and Jews effective political and religious equality with Muslims. This overturned the foundations and structure of Muslim society that had been in place for centuries.

As already stated, Muslims, Christians, and Jews are all regarded as "People of the Book," believers in God, revelation, and the Day of Judgment. As such, Christians and Jews were not persecuted or forced to become Muslims. No attempt was made to subject them to the Muslim legal code—they were left free to regulate their own communal and personal lives in accordance with their own religious laws. At the same time, however, they did not enjoy equal status with their Muslim counterparts. In fact, they were considered a special category within Muslim society and were referred to as *dhimmis*, or non-Muslims. Literally, this term meant "wearers of the belt." They were protected people not required to perform military service (although some did). They also were expected to pay specified taxes, such as a poll tax paid by all non-Muslim males.

European intervention turned this world upside down. The improved status of Christians and Jews seemed to many Muslims to be instigated by hostile forces that sought to weaken Muslim control over lands they considered to be their own. Muslim resentment toward Christians was further intensified because European consuls and traders hired Christians to represent them in the selling of machine-made European goods that were cheaper than the products sold by Muslim merchants. The hired Christians also were offered foreign citizenship, which afforded them protective status, evasion of local taxes, and exemption from Muslim authority.

The local market the Muslims relied on thus was undermined to the benefit of Europeans and their Christian protégés. What made matters worse was the manner in which some Christian clergy flaunted their newfound equality, by holding public processions in elaborate vestments amid ringing church bells—practices that, for centuries, had been forbidden under Muslim law.

INTERVENTION QUICKENS

The process of intervention began slowly during the first decades of the nineteenth century but accelerated by the middle of the century, especially after the Crimean War (1853–1856). The war arose from competition among the "great powers" (Russian, French, British, Ottoman) in the Middle East. It was more directly caused by Russian demands to exercise protection over the Orthodox Christians under Ottoman authority. Another major factor was the dispute between Russia and France over the respective privileges of the Russian Orthodox and Roman Catholic churches in the holy places in Palestine.

The Crimean War was managed and commanded poorly on both sides. Disease accounted for a disproportionate number of the approximately 250,000 men lost by each side. Marking the war's conclusion was the signing of the Treaty of Paris on March 30, 1856, which proved to be a major setback for Russia's Middle East policy. The Ottoman Empire, in taking part in the treaty signing, promised to respect the rights of all its Christian subjects. On the surface, it appeared to be a minor concession, but nevertheless, it served to raise the prestige and self-esteem of the Christians living in the Middle East, especially in relation to their Muslim neighbors. In a very real sense, this set the stage for the Jewish immigration, which was less than 30 years away.

As previously stated, the consequences of European intervention were initially small and incremental and later became large and wrenching. Over the course of a century and a half, from the beginning of the nineteenth century to the final destruction of Palestine, the Palestinian people witnessed many great industrial, technological, political, economic, social, and cultural changes. Very few, if any, of the changes were meant to benefit Palestinians. Economic activity and productivity in trade, agriculture, industry, and services increased substantially but became more and more dependent on Europe. In other words, European intervention propelled the people of Palestine from a largely subsistence and semi-feudal existence

When the British decided to take a hands-on interest in Palestine, the effects of their control led to the decline of the region. Although cultural and religious differences were at the center of the problem, issues such as foreigners taking over the local market worried the Palestinians. As European influences began to seep into every aspect of the economy, Palestinians did their best to live a traditional lifestyle *(above)*.

into a market economy completely dependent on European trade and capital investment.

Throughout this transformation, Palestinian peasants clung to their land, their villages, their families, and their identity. Their attempts to preserve their traditional way of life—the only way of life they had known—proved to be futile. Once Europe's intervention had started, it was impossible to stop the tide sweeping Palestine toward its inevitable breakdown. European intervention created the conditions for the dispossession of its people long before the actual creation of Israel and the displacement of Palestinian Arabs in 1948.

Adding to these changes was the small, so-called peaceful crusade of religiously inspired European immigration, investment, and institutional development. More specifically, French Catholics participated in what they called "the peaceful crusade," visiting holy places and donating substantial sums to build religious institutions. The German Templars established agricultural colonies with the idea of settling in Palestine and Christianizing it, if possible. Protestant missionaries from Europe and the United States also went to Palestine. They sought converts among members of other Christian sects and, in a few cases, encouraged Jewish immigration. As evangelical Christians who considered the end of the world to be close at hand, they hoped to bring Jews to Palestine and to convert them to Christianity in the Holy Land prior to the Day of Judgment.

GROWING NATIONALISM

Just as important was the rise of modern education, which was accompanied by drastic changes in social values, norms, and lifestyles. Following these changes, and perhaps even inspired by them, was the birth of Arab and Palestinian nationalism and the strengthening and spreading of the Islamic consciousness via the rise of the press. Historically, various technological, cultural, political, and economic advances have fostered nationalism, since improvements in communication extend the awareness of people beyond their villages and provinces. This spread of education gives people a feeling of a common background and participation in a common cultural heritage. Cultural identification gives people a sense of helping to determine their fate as a nation and of sharing responsibility for the future well-being of that nation. All of this occurred in Palestine in the context of a rapidly increasing population, both from natural increase and, to a lesser extent, because of the immigration of European Christians and Jews, which drastically altered the composition of the country.

Looked at in this context, Arab and Palestinian nationalism is partly a reaction to European intervention. After all, it was European intervention that transformed the economy, created new social classes, and rearranged power relationships among groups. European intervention also introduced the majority of technological, cultural, and political advances. Even though these changes would, in the long run, hasten the demise of traditional Palestinian society, they would, in the meantime, also enable the Palestinians to build a defense against change. In the nineteenth century, their most important defense was their growing sense of nationalism.

This growing sense of self-awareness should not be underestimated. In their history, culture, and religion, Palestine and the Palestinians have long been an integral part of the Arab and Islamic world. For centuries, the country and its people have been the geographical and social bridge connecting the *Mahriq* or "Arab East" to Egypt and the *Maghreb* or "Arab West." Palestinians are related by kinship, as well as by economic, religious, and political ties, to the people of Lebanon and Syria to the north, Jordan and Iraq to the east, Saudi Arabia to the southeast, and Egypt to the west.

Arab patriotism was still in its infancy during the early part of the nineteenth century. Over time, it steadily picked up momentum, especially in the latter half of the century and the first decades of the twentieth century. By the time of the destruction of Palestine and the dispersal of its people, Palestinian nationalism had become of central importance, influencing the politics and economics of the eastern Arab world. In fact, this sense of self-awareness, along with the so-called "Palestinian question," has become an important factor in

The Dome of the Rock in Jerusalem is considered one of the most holy sites in both Judaism and Islam. Muslims believe this spot *(above)* is the place where the prophet Muhammad rose toward heaven on a winged horse, but Jews claim that this is the location of several important events in Jewish history. Because both groups have such strong ties to the area, the Dome of the Rock, located on the Temple Mount in Jerusalem, has become one of the most contested sites in the world.

conflicts between states in the region, and also between opposing political groups, regimes, and the people within many
states. The issue of Palestine has become central to both non-
religious and religious political and social movements.

As stated earlier, this awakened nationalism among Arabs and
Palestinians was accompanied by a rise in Islamic consciousness.
In fact, one of the most powerful ideological concerns regarding
Palestine involves religion. Islam views Palestine as sacred and
Hebron and Jerusalem as sacred cities. Islam's religious text, the
Koran, refers to the country as *al-Ard al-Muqaddasah*, meaning
"the Holy Land." The Ibrahimi Mosque in Hebron is the site of
the grave of the prophet Abraham (*Ibrahim* in Arabic). Jerusalem
is the site of al-Haram al-Sharif (the Noble Sanctuary) on the
Temple Mount, the third holiest shrine of Islam after Mecca and
Medina. The Noble Sanctuary includes al-Masjid al-Aqsa and the
Qubbat al-Sakhra (Dome of the Rock) mosques. Jerusalem and
the Holy Land of Palestine are powerful symbols of identity for
Muslim individuals.

Following the Crimean War, Palestine became even more
vulnerable to European intervention. From about the middle of
the nineteenth century to the beginning of World War I, European colonists settled in Palestine in small numbers, which
sped up the integration of the country's economy into the
European method. At first, small numbers of Muslim immigrants entered the country from old Ottoman territories: There
were North Africans fleeing French colonization in Algiers and
Morocco, Bosnians fleeing Austrian repression in Yugoslavia,
and Circassian refugees fleeing the Russians. These immigrants
arrived in relatively small numbers and assimilated quickly
into the culture and society of Palestine, which was important
for the stability of the region.

Unlike their Muslim counterparts, Christian and Jewish
immigrants had a different motivation for going to Palestine.
They went, not as refugees seeking sanctuary, but as Crusaders, Salvationists, and Redeemers. They went to "rescue" the
Holy Land. For example, the *Tempelgesellschaft*, or "Association

of Templars," a Protestant Piestic religious movement from the German kingdom of Wurttemberg, went to Palestine to "rescue humankind from the anti-Christian spirit." Their leaders preached the creation of "the people of God," and they assembled in Jerusalem to regain control of Palestine as heirs to the Promised Land.

3

The Rise of Zionism

Zionism is a nationalist movement created to unite the Jewish people of the Diaspora and to settle them in Palestine, the ancient homeland of the Jews. The Diaspora refers to the expulsion of Jews from the Holy Land and their scattering across other parts of the world. Zionism was born in the latter half of the nineteenth century. The movement's name comes from the word *Zion*, the ancient Hebrew name for the easternmost hill of the city of Jerusalem, known today as the Temple Mount. In 1000 B.C., King David captured Zion and made it the center of the political and cultural life of the ancient Hebrews. Eventually Zion became a designation for all of Jerusalem and Palestine. After the fall of Judea in A.D. 70, Zion became the symbol of the hope that the Jewish homeland in Palestine eventually would be restored. Over the centuries, the Jews of the Diaspora associated the hope of return with the coming of the Messiah, a savior whom God would send to deliver them.

THE SPREAD OF ANTI-SEMITISM

Prior to the nineteenth century, small numbers of Jews often migrated to Palestine to join Jewish communities that continued to exist there, but they remained a small minority among a largely Palestinian Arab population. In the latter half of the nineteenth century, however, this all changed. It was during this period that the modern Zionist movement was born. It was inspired primarily by the rise of nationalism and anti-Semitism in Eastern and Central Europe. In the second half of the century, organized anti-Semitic parties emerged in Germany and Austria-Hungary.

Anti-Semitism was a serious problem in Russia too. The assassination of Tsar Alexander II in 1881 unleashed a wave of nationalist and anti-Jewish feelings and violence there. The tsar was killed with a bomb thrown by a member of the Narodnaya Volya, or "Land and Freedom" movement, a nineteenth-century Russian revolutionary organization that regarded terrorist activities as the best means of forcing political reform. The assassin was not Jewish, but rumors spread that Jews were responsible for Alexander's death. As a result, mobs in more than 200 cities and towns attacked Jewish people and destroyed their homes and property. By the beginning of World War I, a vast migration movement of more than 1.5 million Jews had left Russia. The great majority headed for the United States, while others set their sights and hopes on Palestine.

This first wave of immigration took the name of *BILU*, which comes from a passage in the Bible that reads, "*Bet Ya'acov lechu ve nelcha*" or, "O House of Jacob, come ye, and let us go." The efforts of Zionism to colonize Palestine usually are dated from the arrival of the *Biluim*, the people who initiated the first of five identifiable waves of Jewish immigration to Palestine in modern times.

Some other Russian Jews also began to think about migration to Palestine during this period. Many turned to the ideas being advanced by intellectuals such as Moshe Leib Lilienblum and Leo Pinsker, who were the major contributors to Zionist thought and ideology during this initial phase. In *Let Us Not Confuse the Issues*, Lilienblum wrote, "Let us gather our dispersed from Eastern Europe and go up to our kind with rejoicing, whoever is on the side of God and his people, let him say, 'I am for Zion.'" Leo Pinsker stated similar themes in his widely read pamphlet *Auto-Emancipation: An Appeal to His People by a Russian Jew*. Although Palestine was less central in Pinsker's thinking, he embraced the idea of Jewish nationalism and pleaded for a Jewish national home.

The writings of these two men and others became the philosophical foundation for such organizations as the Hovevei

The first mass migration of Jews to Palestine was after the assassination of Tsar Alexander II in 1881. Large mobs attacked homes and businesses, and half the Jewish population left Russia for the Middle East. Baruch Alter *(above)* was 84 years old when he was able to use his savings to leave Eastern Europe and live on an agricultural commune in Palestine.

Zion, a name that means the "Lovers of Zion." Lilienblum even became a leader of the Hovevei Zion movement, which collected money, offered courses in the Hebrew language and Jewish history, and provided instruction in self-defense, all of which were viewed as preparation for immigration to Palestine.

Although less violent at the time than tsarist Russia, Western and Central Europe also experienced a rise in anti-Semitism. In

Germany, for example, economic hard times led to charges that the country was being undermined by corrupt Jewish financiers. In response to the involvement of some Jews in the many financial scandals that were uncovered, an onslaught of anti-Semitic literature began to appear. The very term *anti-Semitism* was coined in 1879 by the German agitator Wilhelm Marr to designate the anti-Jewish campaigns then underway in Central Europe.

Anti-Semitism also was on the rise in France, which set in motion several events that would have a direct impact on the Zionist movement. One of these critical events was the trial and conviction of Captain Alfred Dreyfus, a Jewish officer who had risen to a high position in the French army. In 1894, he was accused of spying for Germany and, as a result, was court-martialed and imprisoned. Later, because of irregularities during his trial, he was retried and then, though still found guilty, granted a pardon. Finally, after 12 years, he succeeded in proving his innocence, winning an appeal before the high court and gaining reinstatement in the army.

Although many non-Jews, such as Emile Zola, believed in Dreyfus's innocence and worked to clear his name, the incident nevertheless had obvious anti-Semitic overtones. When Dreyfus was stripped of his rank and expelled from the National Military Academy, he was greeted by clenched-fist crowds screaming *"à bas les Juifs,"* meaning "down with the Jews." The Dreyfus affair was shocking to many Jews because France had long been regarded as hospitable to those of the Jewish faith. For many European Jews during the nineteenth century, the scene confirmed their growing belief that anti-Semitism would never disappear and that Jews would never become full-fledged citizens of Europe.

One of the advocates of this point of view was Theodor Herzl, a Hungarian-born Jewish writer and journalist. He is regarded as the most influential organizer of the movement that led to the creation of the state of Israel. In fact, Herzl is considered the founder of modern political Zionism. In February 1896, he published *Der Judenstaat,* translated as "The Jewish State," which soon became the manifesto of the emerging Zionist movement. Herzl was the first to call for immediate political action with international backing. To help implement his plan, he convened a Zionist congress, which met in Basel, Switzerland, in 1897. As a result of the congress, Palestine was chosen as the site of the future state because of its association with Jewish history. The World Zionist Organization also was established to help lay the political and economic foundation for the proposed state.

JEWISH SETTLEMENT OF PALESTINE

Initially, Palestinian Arab reaction to Jewish settlement and the purchase of land was sporadic and impulsive, but over time it became more conscious, political, and sustained. The earliest Jewish settlements soon faced individual attacks by Arab peasants who had been deprived of their land by Jewish settlers. The first formally recorded act of Palestinian opposition was in the form of a telegram signed by several Palestinians and sent from Jerusalem to Istanbul. It urged the Ottoman authorities to prohibit Russian Jews from entering Palestine and acquiring land. This is significant because most of the land obtained by Jewish settlers was purchased from two sources: either from the Ottoman government or from often-absentee land owners who, partly because of the economic trends cited in Chapter 2, needed money. Few Palestinian peasants sold the land that they had long cultivated under their traditional system of land ownership. With the Jewish migrations, the Palestinians either were evicted or transformed into laborers on land they no longer had any control over. Thus began a process that would erupt into violent confrontation time and time again.

When formal appeals to the authorities failed, unofficial opposition to Zionism began to express itself more spontaneously, more directly, and more forcefully. Aside from physical confrontations, a steady stream of written appeals was sent

The Hashomer *(above)* was organized by Jewish settlers to protect their settlements in Palestine. As the Ottoman government began selling off Palestinian land to Jewish organizations and foreign individuals, Palestinians protested and filed formal complaints. When this proved ineffective, local Arabs resorted to violent attacks against the new settlements.

to Ottoman authorities protesting the sale of land to Zionist settlers. Najib Nassar, the editor of the city of Haifa's newspaper *al-Karmel,* was arrested (but later acquitted) for disturbing the peace with the inflammatory nature of his articles opposing the sale of land to Zionist settlers. His attitude reflected the increasing fear, concern, and resentment that Palestinians experienced during the years before World War I.

The sale and purchase of land became a constant source of tension between these two competing groups. While the majority of Jewish immigrants clustered in Palestinian cities, some attempted to establish agricultural settlements. By 1908, there were 26 such colonies with 10,000 members on 400,000 *dumums* of land, an equivalent of 100,000 acres (about 40,500 hectares). Private individuals bought much of the land that was purchased in the early years. Increasingly, however, the Jewish Colonization Association (JCA) and the Jewish National Fund (JNF) purchased the larger estates. These lands were held "in trust" for the Jewish people as a whole.

ARAB OPPOSITION TO LAND SALES

By 1910, Palestinian newspapers and the public at large were vocally outraged over the sale of land totaling 24,000 *dumums* (about 6,000 acres or 2,400 hectares) between Nazareth and Jenin. A rich Lebanese merchant named Emile Sursoq sold the lands to the JCA. The governor of the Nazareth district attempted to prevent the exchange, but he failed. In 1913, Sursoq sold another 22 *dumums* in Marj Ibn Amer to the JCA, which displaced hundreds, if not thousands, of Arab families.

One of the earliest Arab documents written in opposition to the Zionist movement was a book by Najib Azouri, a Christian Arab who had studied in France and then served in the Ottoman administration in Jerusalem. His *Le Reveil de La Nation Arabe* (*The Awakening of the Arab Nation*) called for the separation of Arab provinces from Ottoman rule and predicted violent clashes in Palestine between the Arabs and the Jews for control of the area. Specifically, he wrote:

> Two important phenomena, of identical character but never-theless opposed, which till now have not attracted attention, are now making their appearance in Asian Turkey: these are the awakening of the Arab nation and the latent efforts of the Jews to re-establish, on an extremely large scale, the ancient

kingdom of Israel. These two movements are destined to struggle continuously with one another, until one prevails over the other. The fate of the entire world depends on the result of this struggle between the two peoples, which represent two contradictory principles.

4

Britain Enters the Palestine Question

The beginning of World War I on August 1, 1914, ended an extended period during which the colonial powers of Europe usually had avoided outright warfare. Since the Franco-Prussian War of 1870 to 1871 and the Russo-Turkish War seven years later, peace through diplomacy had been the guiding principle that prevented the European powers from plunging into the depths of catastrophe. Even so, many of the past grievances and resentments continued to fester just beneath the surface of this strained diplomacy.

The French still hoped to avenge their defeat at the hands of the Prussians in 1871, and they remained deeply suspicious of British colonial ambition not only in the Middle East, but in Africa as well. Russia continued to view Ottoman territories, especially Constantinople, as lands they hoped to rule over in the future. Great Britain, still the dominant power, desired to maintain the status quo, and hence the territorial integrity of the Ottoman Empire, if only to use it as a buffer and as a guardian of Great Britain's main routes to India.

UNITING AGAINST A COMMON ENEMY

In spite of their mutual mistrust, however, Great Britain, France, and eventually Russia became allies before 1914. They established an *entente cordiale*, or "cordial understanding." This diplomatic relationship reflected their fear of a common enemy more than a sincere trust in one another's motives. The common enemy in this case was Germany, whose industrial and military expansion since the 1880s, coupled with its global ambitions to acquire colonies, alarmed the other colonial powers. Consequently, Great Britain resolved its dispute with France over African colonies so that together they might restrain Germany. Likewise, Great Britain settled its outstanding conflicts, especially regarding Persia (present-day Iran).

The British believed that Germany had gained too many concessions from the Ottomans, and that this threatened British colonial interests. The most significant gain was the construction of a railway from Constantinople through Anatolia and Iraq to Basra and to the Persian Gulf. British officials considered southern Iraq to be an important area to hold under military and commercial influence.

The British also wanted the area as part of a defense perimeter, protecting civilian and military personnel working in the oil fields of southwest Iran. There also was evidence of large oil deposits in northern Iraq that would prove vital to British economic and political stability. Great Britain controlled the Iranian fields, which were vital to its military position in Europe and Asia. Beginning in 1912, the British navy ran strictly on oil, the majority of which came from the Middle East, particularly Iran.

Great Britain feared any German challenge to its colonial supremacy. By taking into account this British strategic self-interest (often harmful to the region's people), one can begin to analyze the nature of the promises and pledges made to the Arabs and to the Jewish settlers during the course of World War I and through its aftermath. One also can begin to understand how the situation radically transformed the nature and future of the Middle East.

The population of Palestine was caught like pawns in this competition, and the people suffered immensely during the carnage of World War I. The Ottomans arrested both Arab nationalists and Zionist leaders, executing many of the Arab prisoners. The majority of the Jewish leaders were given a choice: prison or exile. As a result, Arab protest in Palestine was stifled and Zionist leaders went into exile. The most notable among these Zionists were David Ben-Gurion, who later became Israel's first prime minister, and Yitzhak Ben-Zvi, Israel's second president.

During World War I, the famed T.E. Lawrence, also known as "Lawrence of Arabia," helped organize an Arab guerrilla campaign against the Ottoman Empire. With Lawrence's help, the British army was able to take Jerusalem in 1917 *(above)* and had complete control over Palestine in 1918.

There was yet more to the suffering of the Palestinians during this time. Since Palestine was used as a military base for the Ottoman army, food was in short supply, crops and livestock were commandeered to feed hungry troops, and trees were cut down and used as a source of fuel for the Ottoman railroads. Also, thousands of Arab peasants were drafted to serve in the military, which further added to already heavy burdens.

By the time the Ottoman Empire collapsed and British forces took control of Palestine in the first half of 1918, the country was in a state of chaos. Hunger was rampant throughout the countryside as well as in the urban areas, and many people were on the brink of starvation. In the Middle East and particularly in Palestine, World War I would prove to be a crucial event that, along with the collapse of the Ottoman Empire, would direct the destiny of the Arab world in the twentieth century.

CONFLICTING PROMISES

Starting in 1915, Great Britain entered into three separate agreements: with the French government, with Sharif Hussein of Mecca (the leader of the Arab revolt against the Ottoman authorities), and with Lord Rothschild, who was the leader of the Zionist movement in Britain. These were the Sykes-Picot Agreement, the McMahon-Hussein Agreement, and the Balfour Declaration, respectively. All three of these agreements were to have explosive consequences for the Palestinian struggle for independence.

Although the British Empire had long protected the Ottomans, when World War I started the Ottomans signed an alliance treaty with Germany against the *entente* powers. The Ottomans also stirred up pan-Islamic feeling, threatening British rule in India (which included what are now Pakistan and Bangladesh). During the war, Great Britain fought back, encouraging Arabs to counter the Ottomans' pan-Islamic campaign and to join in the fighting on the side of Great Britain, France, and Russia. In return for Arab support in the war effort, Great Britain promised certain paybacks.

These promises resulted in an agreement—spoken rather than signed—between Sharif Hussein and Sir Henry McMahon, the British high commissioner for Egypt and the Sudan. Specifically, the British offered to support Arab independence in exchange for their allegiance during the war. Hussein and McMahon exchanged eight letters in which their agreements were specified. For example, in a letter to Hussein written on October 24, 1915, McMahon wrote that, "Great Britain is prepared to recognize and support the independence of the Arabs in all the regions within all the limits demanded by the Sharif of Mecca."

Hussein and other Arabs viewed this agreement as the basis for a united Arab kingdom in the former domains of the Ottoman Empire, including Palestine. (Later, this would be highly controversial, as many argued that Palestine was, like Lebanon, excluded from the correspondence.) In keeping with this agreement, the Arabs gave valuable help to the British by seizing the port of Aqaba. This made it possible to attack Ottoman forces in Palestine from the southeast, as well as from Egypt. The Arabs also prevented the Germans from establishing a submarine base in the Red Sea.

Palestine came under British control in December 1917. British troops under General Edmund Allenby conquered the area and established a military administration called the Occupied Enemy Territory Administration, or OETA. Ironically, the Arab and Palestinian military support was what made it possible for the British to defeat the Ottomans in Palestine and to successfully set up a military administration there.

In the meantime, the British made a deal with the French government known as the Sykes-Picot Agreement. This agreement divided the Ottoman territories between Great Britain and France. Under the arrangements, France would have direct authority in coastal and northern regions of Syria, and Great Britain would control Iraq, Transjordan, and the port cities of Haifa and Acre. Palestine would be placed under an international administration made up of Great Britain, France, and

Russia, and representatives of the Sharif of Mecca. The Sykes-Picot Agreement blatantly contradicted the McMahon-Hussein Agreement made almost a year earlier.

Complicating matters further was the Balfour Declaration of November 1917, in which the British government promised to promote Jewish interests in Palestine at the end of the war. This third and final agreement was delivered in the form of a letter from Lord Balfour, the British foreign secretary, to Lord Roth-schild, leader of the Zionist movement in Britain. The content of the letter is very clear:

November 2, 1917

Dear Lord Rothschild,
I have much pleasure in conveying to you, on behalf of His Majesty's Government, the following declaration of sympathy with Jewish Zionist aspirations which has been submitted to, and approved by, the Cabinet. "His Majesty's Government view with favor the establishment in Palestine of a national home for the Jewish people, and will use their best endeavors to facilitate the achievement of this object, it being clearly understood that nothing shall be done which may prejudice the civil and religious rights of existing non-Jewish communities in Palestine, or in any other country." I should be grateful if you would bring this declaration to the knowledge of the Zionist Federation.

Yours sincerely,
Arthur James Balfour

These three contradictory agreements set the stage for post-war conflicts between rising Arab nationalism and Zionist aspirations. Arab and Palestinian discontent erupted into demonstrations in Damascus, Haifa, Baghdad, Jaffa, and Jerusalem between February and April 1920. In Palestine, rising Palestinian and Zionist tensions exploded into demonstrations and rioting during the festival of *Nebi Musa*, a Muslim celebration that

The Balfour Declaration was a letter issued by British Foreign Secretary James Arthur Balfour in support of the creation of Israel within Palestine. Leon Simon, a key member of the Zionist Political Committee, created the initial draft of the declaration (above) at a meeting in London.

happens at the same time as Passover and Easter. Four Arabs and five Jews were killed, and nearly 300 people were wounded.

A British Commission of Inquiry, appointed to investigate the riots and their aftermath, submitted its report on July 1, 1920. It "listed as the causes of unrest in the country: British promises to Arabs during the war, the conflict between these promises and the Balfour Declaration, fear of Jewish domination, Zionist over-aggressiveness, and foreign propaganda."

In spite of the conclusions drawn by the Commission, the British government, headed by Prime Minister David Lloyd George, continued to support Zionist aspirations and the promises made in the Balfour Declaration. On June 30, 1920, Lloyd George appointed Herbert Samuel, a British Zionist, as the first civilian high commissioner of Palestine. To no one's surprise, he supported the building of a Jewish national home in the Holy Land.

5

Arab-Jewish Conflict in the Early British Mandate Period

For the people of the Middle East, the high costs of supporting Great Britain were the result of their faith in British promises that "Great Britain was prepared to recognize the independence of the Arabs in all the regions within all the limits demanded by the Sharif of Mecca." This miscalculated faith in British promises would cost years of turmoil and thousands upon thousands of Arab lives. The British military administration in Palestine (OETA) lasted for 30 months, until June 30, 1920, when it was replaced by a civilian administration headed by Herbert Samuel.

The military administration was bound by international law, and it tried to rule Palestine according to internationally accepted principles found in the *Manual of Military Law*. This manual was the product of two international conventions—the Hague Conferences of 1899 and 1907—organized for the purpose of bringing together the principal nations of the world to discuss and resolve the problems of maintaining universal peace, reducing arms, and bettering the conditions of warfare. Of equal importance for the people of Palestine was the fact that the *Manual of Military Law* obligated "conquering armies" (in this case, the British military) to maintain the status quo of conquered territories until their future had been determined. As a result, the establishment of a Jewish national home was not a top priority for the British military administration, especially when it was confronted with the devastation caused by the war. The military administration also had to consider Arab hostility toward Zionism, which was inspired both by awareness of the Balfour Declaration and by the actions and attitudes of some Zionists. Although these were vital issues that could not be ignored, at the same time, there were other, more urgent concerns.

Because Palestine had served as a staging area and finally as a battleground for Ottoman troops throughout much of the war, the area suffered serious damage to both its land and its people. The Ottomans drafted thousands of local Arab peasants, confiscated Palestinian crops, and decimated entire forests for fuel in the war effort. These developments, coupled with locust plagues and poor harvests due to bad weather and labor shortages in the villages, contributed to an overall sense of chaos and despair. Starvation and disease spread throughout the cities, especially among the poorer inhabitants. No one was spared: not Christian, Jew, or Muslim.

Faced with the enormity of these problems, the British military administration's immediate tasks were to provide food and medical supplies to the people in need and to restore a sense of social and economic order. The administration's policy of maintaining the status quo and of addressing the more urgent needs of the region put them on a collision course with Zionist leaders who were anxious to create a Jewish state. Although the British Parliament strongly favored Zionism, the British military administration's policy was upheld the majority of the time.

For the time being it appeared that the British had found a temporary solution to the impending crisis. Still, this momentary solution was not a permanent answer to certain Zionist requests: participation in the military administration of the country, creation of a land authority that included Jewish experts to survey the region's resources, and formation of an exclusively Jewish military force. The solution certainly did nothing to appease Arab hostility and resistance toward Zionist aspirations, as was pointed out by a member of the military administration: "The antagonism to Zionism of the majority of the population is deep-rooted; it is fast leading to hatred of the British and will result, if the Zionist program is forced upon them, in an outbreak of serious character."

ATTEMPTED SOLUTIONS

In an effort to find a longer-lasting solution to the region's problems, the King-Crane Commission was established in 1919. The commission was named for its two members: Henry C. King, president of Oberlin College, and Charles Crane, a Chicago businessman. At the suggestion of U.S. President Woodrow Wilson, the commission was made to provide an unbiased report of the wishes of the Palestinian Arab people in regards to their future. The commission reported that Arab wishes "were nationalistic, that is to say they called for a united Syria, including Lebanon and Palestine, under a democratic constitution, making no distinction on the basis of religion."

Based on its findings, the commission recommended independence for Syria and Palestine or, failing that, a mandate under the United States—not Great Britain—reflecting the wishes of the Arab people. In regards to Zionist aspirations, the commission recommended "serious modification of the extreme Zionist Program."

The King-Crane Commission's findings were virtually ignored. In fact, the report was not published until 1922, three years after it was written. More importantly, it was not published until a full two years after the future of Palestine and the Palestinians already had been determined by an international conference.

That international conference took place at San Remo, on the Italian Riviera, beginning on April 19, 1920, and lasted six days. Its purpose was to decide the future of the former territories of the Ottoman Empire. The prime ministers of Great Britain, France, and Italy, and representatives from Japan, Greece, and Belgium attended. The conference approved the final framework

After ignoring the King-Crane Commission's recommendation to modify the plan for Israel, world leaders gathered in San Remo, Italy, for a conference to establish the fate of the Middle East *(above)*. The mandates created during the conference led to further foreign intervention in Arab countries, particularly in Palestine, Lebanon, and Syria.

of a peace treaty that obligated the former Ottoman Empire to renounce all rights over Arab Asia and North Africa.

During the conference, several "mandates" were created out of the Ottoman territories in the Middle East. The term *mandate* was used to describe the guardianship of territories formerly held by Germany and the Ottoman Empire. The mandates were placed under the supervision of the League of Nations, and the administration of the mandates was delegated to the victorious powers until the areas could govern themselves.

Two mandates were created out of the old Ottoman province of Syria. The northern half, which consisted of Syria and Lebanon, was placed under the custody of France. The southern half, which consisted solely of Palestine and what would become the Emirate of Transjordan, was put in Great Britain's charge. Iraq also was man-dated to Great Britain. An Anglo-French oil agreement also was concluded at San Remo, providing France with a 25-percent share of the oil revenues generated by the oil fields of Iraq. In exchange, the French agreed not to challenge British claims to Mosul.

"THE OTHER SECTION"

From this point forward, the fate of Palestine and the Palestin-ians was sealed as far as Europe was concerned. Although the stated purpose of the mandate system was to promote the well-being and development of the indigenous population, many critics of the system believed that it was nothing more than a thinly disguised opportunity for the victorious nations to pro-mote their own political, economic, and strategic interests. For example, the text of the British Mandate over Palestine incorpo-rated the Balfour Declaration. The mandate text also contained language giving explicit recognition "to the historical connec-tion of the Jewish people with Palestine" and to the "grounds for reconstituting their national home in that country." Among other references written into the text of the mandate document

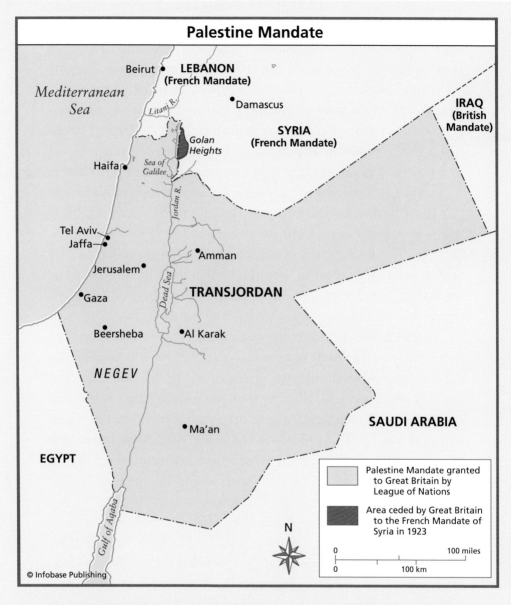

Palestine Mandate

Mediterranean Sea

Beirut • **LEBANON**
(French Mandate)

Litani R.

• Damascus

IRAQ
(British
Mandate)

Golan
Heights

SYRIA
(French Mandate)

Haifa • *Sea of Galilee*

Jordan R.

Tel Aviv
Jaffa

• Amman

Jerusalem •

TRANSJORDAN

• Gaza

Dead Sea

Beersheba • • Al Karak

N E G E V

• Ma'an

SAUDI ARABIA

EGYPT

Gulf of Aqaba

© Infobase Publishing

N

Palestine Mandate granted
to Great Britain by
League of Nations

Area ceded by Great Britain
to the French Mandate of
Syria in 1923

0   100 miles

0   100 km

The San Remo Conference granted mandates for Iraq and Palestine to the British government, while the territories of Syria and Lebanon were given to France *(above)*. Although these Middle Eastern countries were not made into colonies, the French and the British used the acquired land for resources and trade without concerning themselves with the local population.

was a provision stating that "The Administration of Palestine shall facilitate Jewish immigration under suitable conditions and shall encourage close settlement by Jews on the land, including state lands and waste lands not required for public purposes."

While Zionists were pleased with the mandate provisions, Palestinian Arabs were increasingly alarmed. There were numerous references to the "Jewish community," but Arabs and Palestinians, who made up 90 percent of the population, were referred to repeatedly as merely "the other section" of the population.

Further evidence of the Western powers' selfish motives was the fact that the overall postwar settlement conformed closely to the arrangement set forth in the secret Sykes-Picot Agreement of 1916. The French had obtained their strategic objectives by taking Syria and Lebanon, and the British were in control of the territories they deemed essential for the protection of their self-interests. Compared to Iraq, which had an unlimited supply of oil, Palestine was a poor country lacking in resources, as well as investment and growth potential. Nevertheless, it was of strategic importance to the British schemes in the Middle East. The country was the primary buffer state in Great Britain's defense of the Suez Canal, which was the shortest sea route to India. Palestine also was in the air routes to India and Iraq. More important than that, Palestine would become a primary terminus of the oil pipelines from Iraqi oil fields, which would be operated by the British-owned Iraq Petroleum Company.

The San Remo Conference led to political tension not only in Palestine, but in Syria, Lebanon, and Iraq as well. In Palestine, the renewal of Jewish immigration following the San Remo Conference inflamed tensions between the Arab and Jewish communities. Palestinians saw the arrival of 10,000 Jewish immigrants between December 1920 and April 1921 as a dreadful omen of what the future would bring if the flood were not halted.

The Jewish presence in Palestine seemed likely to prevent the country from evolving into an independent Arab state. At the same time, the mandate gave England extensive powers—virtually life and death decisions—over the people of the region. These included legislative and administrative authority and responsibility for Palestine's foreign relations, domestic security, and defense. England also was entitled at all times to use the roads, railways, and ports of Palestine for the movement of armed forces and the carriage of fuels and supplies.

After the establishment of the mandate system, questions arose in politically active circles as to who would control the former Ottoman territories. In Palestine, the question was to what degree Arab and Jewish political rights would be respected. Increasingly, Palestinians found themselves in a position of being disenfranchised, dispossessed of their dreams of independence, and, in some cases, dispossessed of their lands. They lived under the rules and regulations of British strategic self-interest.

Even though Arabs were the majority population group in Palestine, no Arab was nominated to head government posts. The percentage of Arab representation in government was less than their percentage of the total population. Their minimal inclusion still excluded them from government positions in which they could fight against the mandate system. Typically, a qualified Arab was given a position of responsibility only if British officials were looking to save money, because Arab personnel received lower salaries.

As far as the mandate system was concerned, circumstances for Jews were quite the opposite. They were not subjected to the same personal or economic disadvantages. Their salaries were higher, and their government participation was a means of furthering Zionist objectives, which they advocated. In situations in which British officials had made important decisions regarding issues important to the Jewish community, Zionists often could rely on an official who was at least sympathetic to the Zionist cause, if not a committed member of the movement.

As the mandate system became more established, Palestinian Arabs found themselves in a position of being written out of their own history. They were reduced in status from the majority population of Palestine to that of "the other section" of the population. These developments set the stage on which Arab and Zionist conflict was to evolve in Palestine during the years between the two World Wars.

6

The Beginning of Open Palestinian Resistance

The first sign of Palestinian discontent with the British administration happened during the Nebi Musa festival celebration in April 1920. The disturbance was triggered by a confrontation between Palestinians and a procession of Jews. A British-appointed commission investigated the incident, but no recommendations or findings were ever published.

Riots also erupted that May, first during a celebration on May Day 1921. Most of the Palestinian and Arab discontent that was expressed during this disturbance was in the aftermath of the San Remo Conference. Later in May, a rebellion erupted in Iraq and lasted throughout the summer, followed by disturbances in several other parts of the region. There were 47 Jews and 48 Arabs killed, and 214 people were wounded. British soldiers defending Jewish settlements killed numerous Palestinians.

APPEALS TO LONDON

Palestinian Arabs also tried more peaceful and diplomatic ways of addressing their problems. In August 1921, a delegation led by Musa Kazim al-Husayni, a leading Arab notable from Jerusalem, carried their protests to London. The delegation included both Muslims and Christians. It spent nearly a year negotiating with the British and even visited the League of Nations in Geneva, Switzerland, to protest the plight of the Palestinians and Arabs in general. Their one unyielding demand was that the Balfour Declaration be overturned. The group presented its arguments in a booklet titled *The Holy Land: The Moslem-Christian Case Against Zionist Aggression.*

In response to the delegation's diplomatic efforts, the British made it clear to the Palestinians that the Balfour Declaration would continue to be a guiding principle directing British efforts to govern the region and the people who lived there. The British did, however, encourage further discussion regarding Arab fears of Jewish immigration and the sudden rise of Jewish political power in Palestine after the war and the San Remo Conference.

In February 1922, then–Colonial Secretary Winston Churchill presented the Palestinian delegation with a draft of the constitution that Herbert Samuel had promised the previous summer. This new constitution stated that the future British Mandate government in Palestine would consist of a legislative council composed of the high commissioner, 10 appointed British officials, and 15 local representatives. Of these representatives, 9 would be Muslim, 3 Christian, and 3 Jewish. Despite the relative generosity of the draft constitution, the delegation rejected it, stating that they would not discuss any constitutional arrangements as long as the Balfour Declaration remained the basis for British policy.

Under growing pressure, the British issued a report providing an official interpretation of the Balfour Declaration and clarifying British policy toward Jewish immigration. It was their hope that the explanations would be acceptable not only to Palestinian leaders but also to mainstream Arab opinion. Palestinian leaders flatly rejected the document, though, stating that its endorsement of the principles of the Balfour Declaration made it unacceptable, in spite of some provisions that addressed Arab concerns. Despite this response, Churchill signed the document, and it was approved by the British parliament early in July 1922. It provided Great Britain's official interpretation of the British Mandate in Palestine, pending the formal approval of the League of Nations.

In particular, the Palestinian leaders opposed the report because it affirmed that Jews were in Palestine "as a right and not on sufferance." This meant that the Jewish claim to Palestine was as valid as the Arab claim, and that Jews did not require the permission of the Palestinian people in order to occupy territory within the region. Even more crucial, as far as the Palestinian position was concerned, was the assertion that "the existence of a Jewish National Home in Palestine should be internationally guaranteed" and "formally recognized to rest upon ancient historic connection." The new interpretation did explicitly deny the intention of creating a Jewish state, but from the standpoint of British policy, it also completely undermined the idea of Palestinian authority in the region. Once again, by intent or by accident, British intervention had served the cause of reducing the status of the indigenous Arab population of Palestine and had cast them permanently in the role of the "other."

WAVES OF IMMIGRATION

Although their efforts in Great Britain had been frustrated, Palestinian leaders continued to search for effective means to exercise their rights as a free and independent people and ways to express their discontent and resentment when these rights were denied. Of all of their frustrations, the two most important issues to emerge or reemerge in the aftermath of World War I and the British Mandate were Jewish immigration and the acquisition of land.

In regard to the first important issue, Palestine in 1882 had a small, national Jewish community, or *Yishuv*, as Israeli and Western Jewish historians call it. At that point, the total Jewish population was about 24,000, compared to roughly 500,000 Palestinian Arabs. The size of the Jewish community increased in Palestine from 1882 through several distinct periods of immigration called *aliyahs* ("waves"). The first, consisting of about

The rising anti-Semitism in Eastern Europe caused a wave of Jewish immigration into Palestine. In 1929, anti-Jewish laws in Poland, immigration quotas in the United States, and a troubling economy sparked the fourth massive migration of Jews into Palestine *(above)*.

25,000 immigrants, arrived between 1882 and 1903. Most people were fleeing persecution in Russia. The second aliyah arrived between 1904 and 1914. About 35,000 people arrived in Palestine during this period, mostly from Eastern Europe. By the end of this second phase of immigration, the total Jewish population of Palestine was 85,000.

The end of World War I marked the beginning of the third aliyah of Jewish immigration. This continued between 1919 and 1923, and it brought in about 35,000 immigrants, most of whom were from Russia. The fourth aliyah, between 1924 and 1931, brought about 85,000 immigrants, mostly of Polish origin and of middle-class background. The fifth and final phase of Jewish immigration occurred between 1932 and 1938, and it is estimated to have included close to 200,000 individuals. This dramatic increase is due to the rise of the Nazis in Germany and throughout other parts of Europe.

This heavy influx raised the Jewish population in Palestine to an estimated 370,000 people, about 28 percent of the total population. This is a dramatic increase, especially considering that the December 1931 census of Palestine showed that, of 1.4 million people, 84 percent were Arab and 16 percent were Jewish. Based on these figures, the Jewish population had nearly doubled in less than five years. In fact, of the 200,000 who entered Palestine during the fifth aliyah, 174,000 arrived during the four years between 1932 and 1936.

Given these developments, it is not surprising that the Palestinian population felt growing alarm at the staggering increase of Jewish settlers living in Palestine. In a very short span of time, Palestine's cultural, political, and economic composition was completely altered, and it was all against the will of the Palestinian people. This radical change, especially during the years between 1932 and 1936, without a doubt fueled Palestinian discontent and resentment toward Jewish immigration. It would not be long before these feelings of frustration erupted into open rebellion.

LAND DISPUTES

Immigration was not the only cause that created conflict between Palestine's two opposed communities. The second significant issue that frustrated Palestinian hopes of an independent, self-governing Palestine was the issue of land acquisition. Despite the often-quoted Zionist point of view that Palestine was a land without people, the Jewish immigrants, upon their arrival, discovered that not all Palestinian land was uninhabited or readily available. It has been suggested that, as far as Zionist aspirations in regards to Palestine were concerned, land purchase and immigration complemented one another in the pursuit of creating a Jewish majority in as many districts as possible.

Therefore, the first priority in the selection of land for purchase was how it could be used to attain and sustain a Jewish majority. This was important to Zionist aspirations because, should the day come when Palestine would be divided among Arab and Jewish inhabitants, land holdings might well determine the extent and location of territory allocated to Jews. (The division of Palestine was precisely what was proposed by some commissions of inquiry investigating later disturbances.) As a result of Zionist land acquisition, Arabs who worked the land for their livelihoods were forced to leave. Like two trains traveling at uncontrolled speed along the same track from opposite directions, the Arab and Jewish communities were headed toward a terrible catastrophe.

Peasants and the urban poor rioted and used violence against Jewish settlers, but not yet against British authorities. The Palestinian people in towns and villages organized themselves into Muslim-Christian associations, Arab literary clubs, the Higher Islamic Council, and other groups in an effort to resist Zionist aspirations.

POLITICAL ALLIANCES

The Palestinian elite launched a campaign that they hoped would influence British policy: The Palestine Arab Congress, which claimed to represent "all classes and creeds of the Arab people of Palestine," was held in Haifa in December 1920. It elected 22 members called the Palestine Arab Executive, and it joined the top leaders of the two competing notable Arab families of Jerusalem, the Husseinis and the Nashashibis. The political platform of this

Despite suspicions that he had helped stir up conflict during the anti-Jewish riots in Jerusalem, al-Hajj Amin al-Husseini *(center, wearing white turban)* was appointed as the representative for all Palestinians by the British.

movement included the condemnation of the Balfour Declaration and the idea of a Jewish national home in Palestine, as well as the mandate's support of it. The political platform also rejected the idea of mass Jewish immigration into Palestine, but it advocated for the establishment of a national government in Palestine. This last point was significant because Palestine, like Syria and Iraq, was designated by the League of Nations to establish a national government with legislative and administrative structures.

Although the Palestine Arab Executive movement united the rival political clans of the Husseinis and the Nashashibis to speak for all Palestinians, internal rivalries developed within the group. This actually intensified, and served as a means to sabotage, the unity of the group as well as the Palestinian struggle against the Zionists and the British. The deciding factor came when Herbert Samuel appointed al-Hajj Amin al-Husseini as *mufti*, instead of the candidate favored by the Nashashibi family. The mufti was the main legal consultant and caretaker of all Muslim religious properties in Palestine. Al-Hajj Amin also was elected president of the Supreme Muslim Council over his Nashashibi rival.

This was an important position because al-Hajj Amin was in charge of the community's financial resources, the Muslim law courts, schools, orphanages, mosques, and other institutions to which he held the power to appoint and dismiss employees. He expanded welfare and health clinics, built an orphanage, renovated and supported schools, and organized a tree-planting program. His most symbolic act was to renovate two mosques—the al-Aqsa and the Dome of the Rock on the al-Haram al-Sharif in Jerusalem—through an international Muslim fund-raising campaign.

In spite of these achievements, the rivalry between the Husseinis and the Nashashibis still continued. In fact, the Nashashibis attempted to form an opposing power base in the form of the National Party, and they encouraged the creation of peasant parties. The National Party distanced itself from the Palestine Arab Executive by arguing for greater cooperation with the British authorities. They pointed out that opposition to the British Mandate had failed to bring about the desired changes or even to slightly alter British policy in the region. Therefore, it only seemed reasonable, from their vantage point, to work within the system rather than trying to direct change through opposition. These political developments both reflected and fueled the bitter rivalry between the two nationalist factions, which in turn kept the Palestinians from achieving their larger political goals. These divisions would have dire consequences in the decade to come.

7

The Arab Revolt

While the Palestinian elite attempted more traditional methods of resistance, peasant groups were more radical in their approach. For this reason, they were often at the forefront of a violent struggle—first against the Zionists and, later on, against the British authorities. Even more than their elite counterparts, the leaders and members of the peasant groups demanded immediate social and economic relief from the worsening conditions brought about by Zionist aspirations in Palestine. It was the Palestinian peasants and the urban poor who bore the brunt of this onslaught. Because of their dire situation, they had little else to lose. This feeling among poor Palestinians contributed to the increasingly radical and confrontational mood of some. Over time, as other more traditional means failed, this mood began to spread throughout other areas of Arab society.

Violent confrontation largely subsided after the rebellions of the early 1920s. Then, a combination of factors created a highly charged and politically explosive situation. These factors included Jewish immigration and land purchases, and also the economic conditions faced by Palestinians, including unemployment and impoverishment of the urban poor.

RADICAL SHIFTS

Matters came to a head on Friday, August 23, 1929. A confrontation between Arabs and Jews erupted into a bloodbath in which nearly 250 people were killed and almost twice that many were wounded. Fueled by wild rumors and accusations, the violence erupted in Jerusalem and spread to several other cities, including Haifa, Jaffa, Safad, and Hebron. The British finally suppressed the fighting after a week of turmoil.

The British response was to create another committee, the Shaw Commission, to study the causes of the disturbances. The administration also created a second commission, the Hope-Simpson Commission, to conduct a thorough study of the social and economic conditions in Palestine. The Shaw Commission's

After examining the issues that sparked the Jewish-Palestinian riots, the Hope-Simpson Commission published the Passfield White Paper, which discouraged Jewish immigration and land ownership in Palestine. While the Arab groups were wary of the declaration, outraged Jews around the world took up protests against the British government (above).

report, published in March 1930, concluded that the basic cause of the disturbances was the Palestinian people's feeling "of disappointment of their political and national aspirations and fear for their economic future." In particular, the report identified Zionist immigration and land conditions as the primary reasons for the 1929 outbreaks. The commission declared that "a landless and discontented class is being created," and it called for limitations on the transfer of land to non-Arabs.

In the meantime, the Hope-Simpson Commission, headed by Sir John Hope-Simpson, issued a report called the Passfield White Paper on May 27, 1930. It reaffirmed the conclusions reported by the Shaw Commission, for which it came under vigorous attack by Zionists and their supporters in Great Britain and Palestine. This political pressure overwhelmed the minority government of the new British prime minister Ramsay MacDonald. In response to this political pressure, MacDonald wrote a letter to Dr. Chaim Weizmann (a letter that also was published) that in effect rejected and reversed the policy recommendations outlined in the Passfield report.

MacDonald's policy reversal kept in place the exact social, economic, political, and institutional processes that the British administration had determined to be the causes of disturbances in Palestine. For many Palestinians, this confirmed how much power and influence the Zionists exercised over the British government. For a long time, the more radical Arabs had advocated armed resistance, not only against the Zionists but also against the British authorities. In the aftermath of this one final rejection, revolution seemed the only answer. Whether the British knew it or not, they had set in motion what history would remember as the Arab Revolt.

Several important incidents in 1933 and 1935 contributed to the increasingly radical and confrontational mood of the Palestinians. On January 30, 1933, Adolf Hitler was sworn in as chancellor of Germany. He immediately passed laws that barred Jewish participation in professional and commercial activities. The so-called Nuremberg Laws restricted citizenship to Aryans (white gentiles, or non-Jews) and banned marriage between German gentiles and Jews. Because of this rise in government-sponsored anti-Semitism, German Jewish emigration increased dramatically.

A majority of those leaving did not go directly to Palestine. Those who did were able to transfer much of their savings, thanks to an arrangement made between Zionist leaders and the Nazi government. The Nazis were anxious to get rid of their "Jewish

A British soldier guards Arab prisoners before they are taken away to prison. Believing their diplomatic leaders to be ineffective in dealing with the British, young Palestinian men took up arms and organized guerrilla campaigns. The main targets of their violent attacks were Jewish immigrants and the British government.

problem," and they even granted permission to the Zionist orga- nization to establish training camps in Germany to prepare immi- grants for their futures in Palestine. A high-ranking SS officer named Adolf Eichmann was in charge of making these arrange- ments. Eichmann would later be responsible for the murder of millions of Jews during World War II.

German Jewish immigration to Palestine coincided with increased Jewish emigration from Eastern Europe, especially from Poland. The doubling of the Jewish population in Palestine between 1932 and 1936 brought in far more middle-class than working-class immigrants. This allowed for a major infusion of funds into Palestine, whose urban and Jewish sectors underwent an economic boom in the mid-1930s despite the worldwide depression. For the Arab population in Palestine, this new flood of immigrants who were relatively well-off was like pouring salt into old wounds.

Another incident that inflamed tensions between the two communities was the discovery in 1935 of a shipment of guns that had been smuggled into the country. Palestinians believed that Jewish agents had arranged the shipment. Whether this was true or not, it intensified Arab anger and frustration. In that same year, 1935, police killed Sheik Izz al-Din al-Qassam and several of his collaborators. Al-Qassam was president of the Haifa branch of the Young Men's Muslim Association, an important group in both Egypt and Palestine. He had devoted himself to organizing young Arabs for direct action against the Zionist and British authorities. His death made him a martyr to the cause of militant nationalism.

As a leader, al-Qassam was significant because he aligned him- self with the rural peasantry, the urban poor, and the displaced and landless peasants. Qassam's movement was inspired by his concern for social justice and by his belief in direct confronta- tion. Although he was a religious cleric, al-Qassam demanded that the mufti provide money for arms instead of building and renovating mosques. He believed that the diplomatic and politi- cal tactics used by the elite leadership were not only ineffective in obtaining Palestinian rights, but also had brought the country to the brink of disaster.

Al-Qassam was not the only Arab leader who held this view. Numerous pan-Arabists (advocates of unity for all people of Arab origin) and nationalist groups, including the Istiqlal (Independence) Party, were critical of the moderate Palestinian leadership and its diplomatic methods. The leaders of these new militant groups were articulate men such as Awni Abdul-Hadi, Akram Zu'ayter, Izzat Darwaza, and Ahmad al-Shuqayri (who later became the first chairman of the Palestine Liberation Organization, or PLO). They advocated not only strong opposition to the Zionists but, more importantly, against the British Mandate. They wanted to end the mandate and to replace it with an Arab government in Palestine. Such views captured the imagination of the dispossessed and disenfranchised. Following the death of al-Qassam, a large number of young Palestinians formed groups and called themselves Ikhwan al-Qassam, or "Brothers of al-Qassam." They launched an armed struggle against both the Jewish settlers and the British authorities.

THE STRIKE OF 1936

On April 15, 1936, members of the Ikhwan al-Qassam ambushed a bus, killing two Jewish passengers. In retaliation, the Haganah ("Defense"), a Jewish militia created illegally by the Jewish Agency, killed two Palestinians. More counterattacks and paybacks followed, until the British declared a state of emergency. On April 19, 1936, only four days after the bus attack, leaders of the Istiqlal and other nationalist groups responded by announcing a general strike that spread throughout the country. One reason for this strike's success is that it involved middle-class businessmen and professionals in positions of leadership.

Support for the strike came from many different quarters. Eighteen mayors endorsed it, and petitions were submitted by hundreds of senior- and mid-level civil servants. Thousands of workers left their jobs, causing hundreds of businesses to close.

As the strike gained momentum, the half-dozen existing Palestinian parties, which included many members of the political elite, formed a new group to coordinate strike activities. This group had 10 members and was known as the Arab Higher Committee.

The mufti, al-Hajj Amin al-Husseini, was chosen to serve as president. Serving in this capacity jeopardized his position with the British, since they were the ones who had appointed him to political office. But he had no choice, other than joining the militants. The Arab Higher Committee, or AHC, represented all political factions and social sections of Arab society. The AHC advocated the complete end of Jewish immigration, the prohibition of land sales to non-Arabs, and the establishment of a national government responsible to a parliamentary or representative council.

The strike lasted six months. To provide food and other necessities for the strikers, the strike committee operated special distribution centers. Workers also closed the port of Jaffa, and the Supreme Muslim Council closed its school. At first, it was a well-organized and effective act of civil disobedience, but it was not long before civil disobedience turned into armed insurrection. A May Day demonstration in Haifa erupted into a violent confrontation when numerous demonstrators attacked the police, who responded by firing into the crowd. Several people were killed and others wounded. Triggered by these deaths, the Arab Revolt spread into the countryside. Many peasant families contributed men, food, money, and shelter to the cause.

The rebels organized themselves into guerrilla bands made up of a few men with a leader. Guerrillas used hit-and-run tactics, primarily at night and usually in local areas that were familiar to them. As the revolt progressed, the guerrillas operated under a regional or national command structure, especially after the arrival of Syrian military leader Fawzi al-Qawuqji, who would later serve in the crucial conflict of 1947 to 1948.

It was the role of the guerrilla bands to be spontaneous and effective, an act they called *Faz'a*, Arabic for "surprise." Faz'a was used when coming to the aid of other guerrilla bands or forces under fire by British troops. Sometimes it was simply used for sounding the alarm, to alert fellow co-conspirators when British troops were on the move. The local guerrilla bands had the advantage of their small numbers and knowledge of the terrain to escape the British and hide among their kin and fellow villagers.

The general strike formally ended in October 1936, but by this time the country had been plunged into a prolonged period of violent confrontation. The Arab Revolt continued on sporadically until it was interrupted by the outbreak of World War II in 1939. At the conclusion of World War II, the conflict resumed and has continued in various forms until the present day.

8

The Arab Loss of Palestine

Both the strike and the armed insurrection that followed were a direct challenge not only to Zionist aspirations in Palestine but also to British authority. This marked a turning point in the Palestinian Arab struggle for independence. Its significance was not lost on the British. In fact, to counter the revolt, the high commissioner quickly established a series of harsh emergency regulations. Although these measures were designed to calm the tensions caused by the conflict, they merely fueled Arab resentment and hostility.

At that point, the British declared the strike illegal. In late September 1936, after the assassination of a British district commissioner, the administration arrested, jailed, or deported strike leaders and other prominent members of the Arab Higher Committee. They also censored or closed down newspapers, imposed strict curfews, and dealt out harsh punishments to anyone remotely suspected of involvement in militant activities. The British also conducted—without warrants—house-to-house search and seizure operations in an effort to disarm and intimidate Palestinian citizens. This was all in the hopes that the disturbances would be calmed.

THE PEEL COMMISSION

These events also led to another British commission of inquiry. The Palestine Royal Commission, commonly known as the

Peel Commission, was ordered to investigate the causes of the revolt and to explore ways and means of suppressing future Palestinian resistance. Under the direction of Lord Peel, the six-member commission began its investigation in November 1936 and eventually held 66 meetings, more than 30 of them in secret.

In July 1937, the commission published its report. It stated that the causes of the revolt were the same as those that had triggered rebellions in 1920, 1921, 1929, and 1933. Specifically, these causes were "the desire of the Arabs for national independence" and "their hatred and fear of the establishment of the Jewish National Home." The report elaborated, "about 1,000,000 Arabs are in strife, open or latent, with 400,000 Jews. There is no common ground between them." Furthermore, the report stated, rather bluntly, that the British Mandate had not only failed to achieve its prime directive; it had deepened the antagonism between the two communities in Palestine. It was therefore the recommendation of the commission that the mandate should be ended and the territory of Palestine should be partitioned to empower each "national community" to guide its own destiny. This last proposal outraged the Palestinian community because they saw it as a means of dissecting their national homeland.

This was not the only repercussion of the recommendations issued by the Palestine Royal Commission. Not long after the commission published its report, an order was issued for the arrest and detention of al-Hajj Amin al-Husseini, who had chaired the Arab Higher Committee. Al-Husseini was able to escape capture, however, by crossing the border into Lebanon, which was under French mandate. The British also declared as illegal the Arab Higher Committee and several other national organizations. About the only Arab organization allowed to function was the Nashashibis' National Defense Party. This permission from the British, however, destroyed the party's legitimacy in the Arab community.

MORE UPRISINGS, MORE COMMISSIONS

In spite of these setbacks, the Arab Revolt intensified following the Palestine Royal Commission's published report. It reached its climax during the summer of 1938. Numerous Palestinian cities, including Jerusalem, joined this rebellion. In response, the British launched an all-out offensive to crush the uprising. They assembled two divisions of soldiers, squadrons of airplanes, the British police force in Palestine, the Transjordanian frontier forces, and 6,000 Jewish auxiliaries. With these combined forces, the British outnumbered the Palestinian rebels 10 to 1. Nevertheless, the conflict lasted until 1939, when the Palestinian people, having fought as long as they could, finally were overcome by exhaustion. The uprising subsided only after their leaders were in exile and their fighting forces were surrounded. It was an uneasy calm, but this was by no means the end of the struggle. It was just a brief respite.

During the calm that followed the terrible storm of insurrection, the British issued a report called the MacDonald White Paper in May 1939. The report, for the first time during the mandate, reversed its previous policy and made some substantial concessions to Palestinian Arab concerns. Jewish immigration was limited to 75,000 over a 5-year period, and then it would cease unless the Arabs agreed to allow it to continue. Land acquisition was restricted to limited areas, and Palestine would become independent within 10 years if Arab-Jewish relations improved.

Even with these concessions, both the Arab rebels and the Zionists rejected the report proposals. Both felt that the British government had betrayed them. Nevertheless, despite the plan's rejection by both communities, the British implemented it. Because the British government was facing a new world war, the report was seen as a quick solution to a deeply rooted problem. It would prove to be a miscalculation for which the British would pay dearly in the years to come. In the meantime, the world was about to be plunged into war.

In an attempt to stop the riots and violence in Palestine, the British organized military operations to defeat the Palestinian guerrillas. Although British forces had more advanced technology, they were unable to permanently quell the conflicts in the region. Above, Christian Arabs are being searched by British troops as they enter or leave a sector of Jerusalem.

The Arab Revolt of 1936 had won many important concessions for the Palestinian people, but it failed to achieve its principal goal of immediate Palestinian independence. Throughout the next decade, this aim would continue to be frustrated. World War II and the Holocaust, increased Jewish emigration (both legal and illegal) from war-ravaged Europe to Palestine, and growing European sympathy for the Jewish people all contributed to the demise of Palestinian self-determination.

Crucial factors included the increasing influence of the international Zionist movement, especially in the United States. This was coupled with the gradual decline of the British Empire and the emergence of the United Nations. There was an additional problem: the absence of generally respected Arab leaders within Palestine during the 1940s. Although probably no one suspected it at the time, the country and its people were already on the road to disaster.

PALESTINE IN THE FACE OF ANOTHER WORLD WAR

During World War II, the Arabs of Palestine were disorganized and leaderless. In fact, the harsh suppression of the Arab Revolt decimated Palestinian political and military institutions. Nevertheless, the Palestinian people remained as determined as ever to derail Zionist aspirations. There even were some efforts to revitalize the Arab nationalist movement. But the forceful spirit that animated political activism and revolt in the 1930s did not return to full force during the war years.

In contrast, the Jewish community in the 1940s grew economically stronger, and it became tightly organized politically and militarily. With the aid of British training, the Haganah militia—the forces controlled by the Jewish Agency—and other defense militia grew in numbers, skill, and sophistication. In addition, two Jewish terrorist groups rose to prominence: Irgun ("Organization") and the Lohamei Herut Yisrael ("Fighters for the Freedom of Israel"), sometimes referred to as the Lehi and

Stern Gang. Jewish military power was further increased by the experience and technical skill acquired by the 37,000 volunteers in the Jewish Brigade and other units who served in Great Britain's military from the beginning of the mandate. The Jewish community by the end of the war had become strong enough militarily to launch a revolt against the British in 1945 and to conquer Palestine three years later. There was a decisive shift in the balance of power between the two opposing communities: the immigrant-settler Jewish community and the indigenous Palestinian Arabs. This shift would prove fateful.

In 1942, five months after the United States entered World War II, a Zionist conference was held at the Biltmore Hotel in New York City. During this conference, a new Zionist program was announced. This marked a significant turning point in the Zionist struggle to further their aspirations in Palestine. The Zionists were increasingly frustrated with Great Britain because before and during World War II it was strategically necessary for Great Britain to make substantial concessions to the Arab states. As such, the Zionists turned to the United States, the emerging world power, for support.

It was a fruitful moment for the Zionists to air their case to the world, because sympathy toward European Jews had been increasing throughout the world. The conference gave the Zionists and their cause an international forum. In opposition to Britain's 1939 report calling for limits on Jewish immigration and land acquisition, the Zionists demanded open immigration into Palestine and settlement of unoccupied territory. More significantly, for the first time, the Zionists declared publicly their intention to establish a Jewish homeland or commonwealth in Palestine.

Not long after the Biltmore conference, a number of U.S. senators and members of Congress signed a letter to President Franklin Roosevelt supporting Jewish rights in Palestine. In 1944, less than two years later, the U.S. Congress passed a joint resolution endorsing the Biltmore program. The same year, the British Labor Party recommended that their government encourage the immigration of European Jews to Palestine. In August

1945, President Harry S. Truman called on the British prime minister to allow 100,000 European Jews to immigrate to Palestine. This quick succession of events and their profound and lasting consequences marked a death knell for the indigenous Arab inhabitants of Palestine.

In 1946, a year after World War II had ended, the United States and the British government formed a commission to investigate conditions in Palestine. The Anglo-American Commission recommended the conversion of the British Mandate into a trusteeship divided into two autonomous Jewish and Arab provinces, with Jerusalem and the Negev Desert to remain under the control of the British government. Although the British were in favor of the proposal, the Palestinians, the Zionists, and the United States all rejected the plan. The British then also rejected United States and Zionist demands to allow another 100,000 immigrants to enter Palestine.

GREAT BRITAIN TAKES ITS LEAVE

In the meantime, tension between Zionists and the British administration continued to escalate. Local Jews taunted British soldiers and likened them to Nazis. In response, the soldiers, on a number of occasions, entered Jewish settlements and scrawled swastikas and anti-Semitic slogans on their walls.

Increased terrorism by Zionist groups, the majority of it directed against the British, played a significant role in heightening the already seething tension. In 1945, the Irgun attacked two British police stations, leaving nine officers dead. David

(opposite) After the British government handed over the responsibilities of the mandate to the United Nations, the international organization created Resolution 181 to define the borders of Israel and Palestine. Jerusalem and Bethlehem were designated as international territories, and more land was given to Israel than to Palestine.

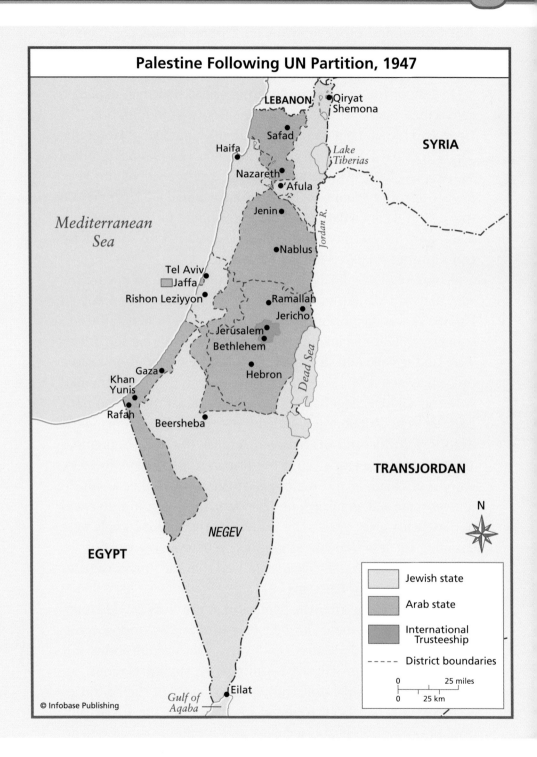

Palestine Following UN Partition, 1947

LEBANON
Qiryat Shemona

Safad

Haifa

Lake Tiberias

SYRIA

Nazareth

'Afula

Jenin

Jordan R.

Nablus

Mediterranean Sea

Tel Aviv
Jaffa

Rishon Leziyyon

Ramallah

Jericho

Jerusalem

Bethlehem

Dead Sea

Gaza

Khan Yunis

Hebron

Rafah

Beersheba

TRANSJORDAN

N

EGYPT

NEGEV

Jewish state

Arab state

International Trusteeship

District boundaries

0   25 miles

0   25 km

Gulf of Aqaba

Eilat

© Infobase Publishing

Ben-Gurion and other mainstream Zionist leaders condemned the attack, but nevertheless, additional attacks followed. In April 1946, seven British soldiers were killed.

In July of the same year, an immense terrorist act exploded across the front pages of every major newspaper in the world. The Irgun had blown up a wing of Jerusalem's King David Hotel that the British used as military headquarters. The explosion killed 91 people—Jews, Arabs, and British. By the end of the year, Jewish terrorist groups claimed to have killed 373 people. Of those, 300 were civilians. In this atmosphere of increasing violence and uncertainty, both the Palestinian Arab and Jewish communities prepared for armed conflict.

It was obvious during the years immediately following the war that British authority in the Middle East, particularly in Palestine, was beginning to erode. After the British failure to suppress the Zionist revolt, it became clearer still that the British were under siege and in retreat. Despite their attempt to restore order between 1945 and 1947, it was a feeble effort compared with the massive assaults they launched against the Palestinians back in 1936. British forces killed 5,000 Palestinians during the Arab Revolt. In contrast, between August 1945 and September 1947, 37 Jewish terrorists and 169 British soldiers died. In 1936, Palestinian leaders and members of the Arab Higher Committee were arrested, detained, or deported, and the committee was outlawed for eight years. The leaders of the Zionist revolt were detained for less than three months. Whatever the reasons for these discrepancies, they clearly showed that the British were no longer in control of Palestine.

Less than a year after the explosion at the King David Hotel, the British government decided to withdraw its troops, relinquish control of Palestine, and turn over responsibility for the mandate to the United Nations. The United Nations, an international organization composed of most of the countries of the world, had been founded in 1945 with the stated purpose of promoting peace, security, and economic development. On November 29, 1947, the UN General Assembly voted for

Resolution 181 on the "Future Government of Palestine," which split Palestine into an Arab and a Jewish state.

In 1947, the Jewish community made up 31 percent of the total population of Palestine. Nevertheless, the UN resolution granted the proposed Jewish state 55 percent of historic Palestine. The proposed Palestinian state, in contrast, was awarded 45 percent of the land of Palestine. Jerusalem and Bethlehem were supposed to be a separate entity under the administration of the United Nations. As expected, Palestinians and other Arabs were outraged and rejected the resolution outright.

THE WAR OF 1948

Palestine was engulfed in war almost as soon as the UN resolution was passed. On November 30, 1947, the day following the resolution, violent confrontations erupted between Arabs and Jews in Haifa, Tel Aviv, Jaffa, Lydda, and Jerusalem. There also was unrest in Beirut, Aleppo, Damascus, Baghdad, and a number of other Arab cities outside Palestine. Al-Hajj Amin al-Husseini had reestablished the Arab Higher Committee in Cairo and then moved it to Beirut. From the Lebanese capital, he declared the UN resolution to be "null and void" and that under no circumstances would the Palestinian people respect it. With British forces in preparation to withdraw from Palestine, the Palestinians used the opportunity to raise a guerrilla army and to resist the implementation of the resolution. A network of local committees supported the guerrillas through fund-raising and recruitment. By March 1948, the guerrillas had been reinforced by the arrival of nearly 7,000 volunteers from neighboring Arab countries. The forces were known as the Arab Liberation Army.

Even with these reinforcements, the Palestinian and Arab forces were severely outnumbered, out-armed, and out-trained. Jewish forces had the upper hand in training, technical knowledge, experience, firepower, and mobility. From the start the Palestinians were unprepared politically and militarily to defend

Outraged over the UN partition of Palestine and Israel, men from neighboring Arab countries flooded into the area to support their Palestinian brethren. Known as the Arab Liberation Army, some of these men overcame personal rivalries in order to contribute to the Palestinian cause. Here, two families mark the end of a bloody feud between their two families in order to concentrate on the battle against Israel *(above)*.

the integrity and unity of their country. Given these circumstances, the outcome of this armed conflict was inevitable.

Beginning in April 1948, the Jewish military launched massive assaults against Palestinian forces. Through terror, psychological warfare, and direct conquest, the Jewish military enacted on the Palestinian people one of the worst defeats in the history of the Palestinians' struggle for independence. Entire villages were destroyed and massive numbers of Palestinians fled or were sent into exile.

On May 14, 1948, the Zionists declared the state of Israel, and 11 minutes later, President Harry S. Truman recognized it as a sovereign nation. With these events, Israel came into existence. For the Jewish people, this was the fulfillment of a Zionist vision. For the indigenous Arab inhabitants of Palestine, this was catastrophic—the beginning of the Palestinian diaspora that would last into the next century.

9

The Palestinian Diaspora

The Arabic word *al-Nakbah* meant the destruction of Palestinian society. It also meant the dispossession, dispersal, and destitution of the Palestinian people, a process that began in the 1800s and ended 148 years later. From a total population of 900,000 Palestinians in areas occupied by Israel, 750,000 became refugees. In a matter of less than a month during the spring of 1948, the lives of generations of families, of mothers and fathers and children, had been completely dispossessed and disrupted. That is the meaning of *al-Nakbah* for the Palestinians: suffering that escapes understanding. One people's victory is another people's death and destruction.

OUT OF PALESTINE

After *al-Nakbah*, the people of Palestine were divided into three distinct but widely dispersed areas. Between 150,000 and 180,000 Palestinians remained in their homes and on the land that became Israel. Another 50,000 people remained behind Arab military lines in east-central Palestine and the Gaza Strip. Finally, more than 750,000 became refugees in east-central Palestine (later known as the West Bank), the Gaza Strip, and neighboring Arab countries. For example, 10,000 Palestinians were given sanctuary in Egypt and another 80,000 went to Syria. In many Palestinian homes around the world, displaced families display olive wood carvings or framed needlework pictures with

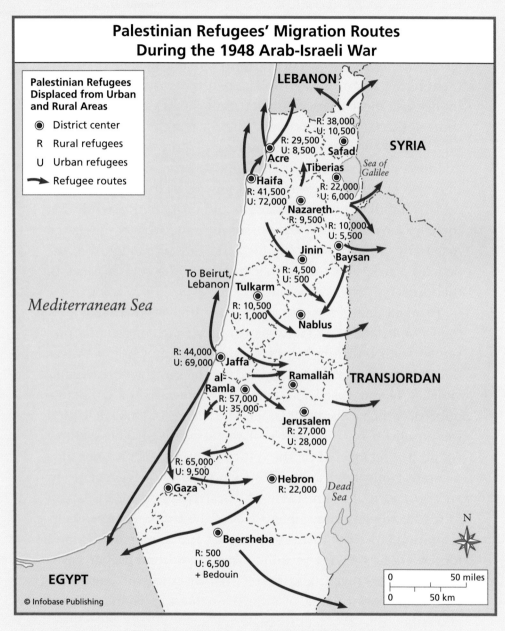

Palestinian Refugees' Migration Routes During the 1948 Arab-Israeli War

Palestinian Refugees Displaced from Urban and Rural Areas

◉ District center
R Rural refugees
U Urban refugees
➤ Refugee routes

LEBANON

SYRIA

R: 38,000
U: 10,500

R: 29,500
U: 8,500 Safad

Acre

Tiberias

Sea of Galilee

Haifa
R: 41,500
U: 72,000

R: 22,000
U: 6,000

Nazareth
R: 9,500

R: 10,000
U: 5,500

Jinin

Baysan

Mediterranean Sea

To Beirut, Lebanon

Tulkarm

R: 4,500
U: 500

R: 10,500
U: 1,000

Nablus

R: 44,000
U: 69,000 Jaffa

al-Ramla

Ramallah

TRANSJORDAN

R: 57,000
U: 35,000

Jerusalem
R: 27,000
U: 28,000

R: 65,000
U: 9,500

Gaza

Hebron
R: 22,000

Dead Sea

Beersheba
R: 500
U: 6,500
+ Bedouin

EGYPT

N

© Infobase Publishing

0   50 miles
0   50 km

Unsure of what awaited them, Palestinian refugees often fled their homes in a rush, without even the necessary items needed for everyday life. Many families left behind land, homes, farms, and traditional heirlooms that had been passed down for generations. These refugees would be spread across the Middle East in various refugee camps *(above)*.

the words *Innana raji'oun* or *Innana 'aidoun*, which means "we shall return."

No matter where they found refuge, the Palestinians who left their homes faced circumstances that added new depths of suffering to an already unbearable crisis. This was primarily because most Palestinians left their homes and villages on short notice, and most assumed their leaving would be temporary, just like it had been many times before when the never-ending conflict between the two opposing communities erupted into violent confrontation. Few, if any, Palestinians realized or understood that this time events would turn out differently. For these reasons, they took few possessions and were not prepared materially or psychologically for a long absence away from the people, places, and things that had been the central focus of their lives only the day before.

To make matters worse, once they had been driven from their homes and their possessions, they were consistently prevented from returning to their communities of origin. It was not only the uncertainties caused by the danger, threats, and violence of war that kept them away, but also the deliberate policies of the new state of Israel. The leaders of Israel defended these policies on the basis that the security of their country would be endangered by the return of hundreds of thousands of Arabs committed to the destruction of the Jewish state. In an effort to make sure these policies remained intact, Israeli forces destroyed many abandoned Palestinian villages, both to prevent Palestinians from returning and to prepare the land for settlement by Jews. In some cases, Palestinian property was needlessly destroyed, and there were instances of large-scale looting and destruction of villages without apparent military necessity.

Without a doubt, the effects of these events were devastating. After a difficult and perilous journey, refugees often found themselves in camps and centers that were ill-equipped to meet their needs. The Red Cross and the Red Crescent, along with numerous other charitable organizations, attempted to bring relief to an ever-increasing population of refugees.

The devastation caused by this diaspora and the effects it had upon the Palestinian people should not be underestimated. Their experiences continue to shape their personal and political outlook. The hardships they faced resonate throughout their art, literature, and political writings like a song of sorrow. Palestinians are driven by a strong and bitter passion to reclaim what they feel belongs to them by birthright. It is the expression of this terrible and painful passion that explodes into vivid, violent images and newspaper headlines. If the past 60 years are any indication, it is also a passion that will not be subdued by bombs and bullets.

NEW FOCUS FOR THE PALESTINIANS

In the years before the dispersal of the Palestinians, the two dominant themes that fueled the conflict between them and the Jewish community were immigration and land acquisition. During the years following the War of 1948, the two most important issues that dominated Palestinian thought and action were concerns regarding the declaration of the state of Israel and the fate of the Palestinian refugees.

From the beginning of this new phase of the conflict, Palestinians and Arabs from other countries argued that the establishment of a Jewish state in Palestine was an illegal and illegitimate act. Palestinians and Arabs who held this point of view likened the Jewish occupation of Palestine to that of a group of strangers who invade and take possession of another person's house. They pointed out that Palestine had been an Arab country for hundreds of years until the organized immigration of Jews from Russia, Eastern Europe, and Western Europe. They also believed that Zionists had orchestrated this mass immigration for the sole purpose of establishing a Jewish homeland, even if that meant dislodging the indigenous inhabitants of Palestine. In the

Palestinian version of the story, the Jews invaded and then occupied the house of the Palestinians against their will, with help from the strategic intervention of the British Empire.

Of course, supporters of the state of Israel offer equally compelling arguments defending the legality and legitimacy of the

The first prime minister of Israel, David Ben-Gurion *(center, with wife)*, arrives in Haifa, Palestine, to bid farewell to the last of the British military in the region. The Palestinians believed the British Empire invaded their country to help Jewish immigrants form an independent nation.

Jewish state. They maintain, for example, that the Jewish people's rights to Palestine come from a historical connection with the land that was established 4,000 years ago, when God granted Abraham and his descendants all the land of Canaan for an everlasting possession. These claims and counterclaims will not be resolved by whoever builds the better case. The relationship, as violent as it has been, is much too complex for so simple a solution.

It is important not to let these arguments obscure the fact that Jewish political rights and statehood have been achieved at the expense of the Palestinian people. Israel is, by definition, a settler colony: when citizens of a foreign country migrate to and eventually take complete control of a new area. The foreign colonizers ordinarily substitute their culture for the existing one. Settlers often exclude native inhabitants from their society or kill many of them in violent confrontations or by exposure to disease. Like other colonized people, such as the Native Americans of North America, the Palestinians cannot reasonably be expected to submit to their dispersal—not to mention their possible political and cultural extinction—without putting up some kind of fight.

This is the basis of the Palestinian argument against the state of Israel. Palestinians believe and are committed to the idea, whether right or wrong, that Palestine by right belongs to its indigenous Arab population, to the Palestinian people, whose presence in their native land was undisturbed for centuries prior to the emergence of modern political Zionism. So far, no arguments, bombs, or bullets have been able to shake the foundations of that belief.

REFUGEE CONCERNS

The second issue that is central to the conflict between the Palestinians and Israelis is the fate of the Palestinian refugees. The Palestinian Arab argument is that, as a result of the War

Pictured, bullet-riddled cacti in the village of Deir Yassin *(above)*. As members of a village determined to live in peace, the people of Deir Yassin agreed to a peace pact with neighboring Jewish villages. Although Deir Yassin's reputation for quiet living was well known, the Irgun attacked the village in the middle of the night, killing 100 women and children.

of 1948, the majority of the Palestinians fled their villages and their land primarily because of the mortal fear created by the systematic terror campaigns executed by the Israeli forces. Palestinians cite Deir Yassin as an example of the terror tactics used by the Zionist forces. Deir Yassin was a Palestinian village about five miles west of Jerusalem. On April 9, 1948, Irgun forces entered the village and massacred 254 defenseless civilians, including 100 women and children. Afterward the bodies were hacked into pieces and thrown into a well. Palestinians claim that, after the massacre, the Irgun command sent out a congratulatory message stating, "As in Deir Yassin, so everywhere, Oh Lord, Oh Lord, you have chosen us for the conquest."

Palestinians believe that the Israelis' motive was to incite panic among the Palestinian population and thereby frighten them to the point of abandoning their land, homes, and possessions. Palestinians also point out that the inhabitants of Deir Yassin were not involved in the war effort. As a matter of fact, Deir Yassin was one of several Palestinian villages that had signed a non-aggression pact with its Jewish neighbors.

It has been estimated that two-thirds of the nearly 9 million Palestinians today are refugees living in dismal camps. Others, though not refugees, nonetheless live under severely restrictive conditions, isolated by walls and fences. It is a condition that many observers consider shockingly similar to the old apartheid regime of ethnic separation in South Africa.

10

Palestinian Authority

The time between al-Nakbah in spring 1948 and the Six-Day War in June 1967 was a period of intense political activity in the Arab world. Political parties and movements spanned the political spectrum from one extreme to the other, from extreme-left parties to conservative movements such as the Muslim Brotherhood. The movement that spoke loudest to most Arabs throughout the Middle East following the destruction of Palestine was secular pan-Arab nationalism.

It is a movement both simple and difficult to define. On the most basic level it is about brotherhood, a belief that Arab people share a common bond and a common origin and should strive together to achieve their common objectives. At the same time, however, it demands something deeper—a belief or philosophy that extends the boundaries of brotherhood to include other people from other countries who share a common or similar historical experience.

During the years in question, the Cold War decades, this movement helped give birth to an even larger movement referred to as the Nonaligned Movement, or NAM. It was a loose association of countries in Africa, Asia, and Latin America. The NAM countries all shared a similar colonial background, and they all refused to align themselves with either one of the world powers at that time: the United States, representing the capitalist or Western bloc, and the Soviet Union, representing the communist or Eastern bloc.

This idea of self-sufficiency and self-determination made a big impact in the Middle East. It gave new meaning to the idea of Arab unity. It meant that the newly independent Arab states had enough shared experiences and interests to make it possible for them to come into close union and cooperation with each other. Such a union would not only give them greater collective power but would bring about moral unity between people and government, which would make government legitimate and stable.

AWAKENED NATIONALISM

Palestinians also listened to the call of pan-Arab nationalism and became actively involved in the struggle to regain their homeland, in spite of the lack of independent Palestinian organizations. The Arab Nationalist Movement (ANM) was founded and organized by Palestinian students at the American University of Beirut in Lebanon. ANM's head was George Habash, who later founded another organization called Popular Front for the Liberation of Palestine, or PFLP.

The Palestinian liberation movement received its greatest boost from the Suez War. Palestinians took part in militia raids that preceded the actual war in 1956. By the mid-1950s, the Egyptian government had become a major supporter of the Palestinian struggle, and it refused to allow Israeli ships to use the Suez Canal. In 1951, Egypt blockaded the Strait of Tiran, Israel's access to the Red Sea, which Israel regarded as an act of war. In July 1956, Egypt nationalized the Suez Canal Company, which had been jointly owned by Great Britain and France. In late October, Israel invaded the Gaza Strip and the Sinai Peninsula. Great Britain and France attacked Egypt a few days later. Although the fighting was brief and U.S. and Soviet pressure forced Israel to withdraw from both the Gaza Strip and the Sinai Peninsula, the conflict further inflamed regional tensions.

For Palestinians, the experience of taking part in this conflict only eight years after al-Nakbah was the push needed to inspire the emergence of an independent Palestinian militant movement. In fact, a popular resistance movement erupted in the Gaza Strip in reaction to Israel's invasion and occupation of the territory during the Suez War. The movement was aided by the military training and technical assistance Palestinians had received from the Egyptian army. As a result, Palestinian rebels launched several successful guerrilla raids across the borders into Israel, similar to the raids Israeli terrorists launched against Great Britain prior to British withdrawal from Palestine.

THE CREATION OF FATAH

Following the success of these initial raids, Palestinians in the Gaza Strip and elsewhere began independent, clandestine campaigns of political organizing, military training, and the creation of social institutions. The most important of the guerrilla groups to emerge in this period was Fatah, also known as the Palestinian National Liberation Movement. The name *Fatah* is an acronym of *Harakat al-Tahrir al-Filastini* (which means Palestinian Liberation Movement), with the order of the initials reversed. Fatah initially was a loose network of Palestinian groups in refugee camps, Palestinian communities, and student groups. Yasser Arafat, Salah Khalaf, Khalil al-Wazir, and Abu Jihad were among its founding members. The movement began to take shape at meetings held in Kuwait in October 1957 but did not come into its full power until several years later, especially after the Six-Day War in 1967. The movement's publication, *Filastinuna*, or *Our Palestine*, first appeared in 1959. Because of its subversive nature, Fatah was forced to operate underground even in Arab states that supported Palestinian liberation.

While Fatah and other guerrilla groups carried out clandestine warfare, al-Hajj Amin al-Husseini, the former mufti of Palestine and president of the Arab Higher Committee, appealed to the League of Arab States to help establish an independent Palestinian state. The League of Arab States, also informally known as the Arab League, is a voluntary association of independent Arab countries. Its stated purposes are to strengthen ties among member states, coordinate their policies, and promote their common interests. The league was founded in 1945 by Egypt, Iraq, Lebanon, Saudi Arabia, Syria, Transjordan, and Yemen. Jordan joined in 1949, as did many other Arab and African countries over the years. The Palestine Liberation Organization became an official member in 1976.

THE BIRTH OF THE PLO

In the meantime, members of the League of Arab States voted unanimously to create a political organization that would speak and act on behalf of the Palestinian people. To initiate this process, the Palestinian Liberation Army came into existence, units of which would be under the jurisdiction and commands of various Arab militaries.

Perhaps even more important was that in January 1964 the first-ever Arab summit was called to discuss Israel's plan to divert the waters of the Jordan River. During this summit, the Palestinian representative of the Arab League, Ahmad al-Shuqayri, was authorized to convene a new Palestine National Council, or legislative congress. The appointed council met in Jerusalem and founded the Palestine Liberation Organization, or PLO, as its executive branch. The stated purpose for the founding of the PLO was to make plans for the establishment of a Palestinian entity that would contribute more broadly to the struggle against the Jewish state—or, indeed, to replace it.

The PLO was founded to establish a more legitimate and organized channel for Palestinian nationalism than that which was offered at the time by independent guerrilla groups. Later, some of these groups, including Fatah, joined the PLO. Professional, labor, and student groups also joined the PLO, but during the course of the organization's evolution, it has been the guerrilla faction that has garnered the most attention from foreigners.

The PLO is made up of three main bodies: (1) the 15-member executive committee, which makes decisions and which includes representatives of the PLO's major guerrilla forces; (2) the 60-member central committee, which is an advisory body; and (3) the 599-member Palestine National Council, which has historically been seen as an assembly of the Palestinian people.

Before the creation in 1993 of the Palestinian National Authority, or PNA, the PLO also had departments and agencies that
provided military, health, information, finance, education, and
other services to the dispersed Palestinian population. Since
1994, however, the PNA has taken over these functions.

The formation of the Palestinian Liberation Organization (PLO) brought together the
independent militias and organized them to reach all aspects of Palestinian life. The
fedayeen, the guerrilla section of the PLO *(above)*, came to have great influence on
the overall group.

The PLO grew in prominence after Israel gained control of the largely Palestinian-inhabited West Bank and Gaza Strip in June 1967. The Six-Day War changed the course of history not only for the Palestinian people struggling to regain their homeland, but for all the independent Arab states throughout the Middle East. It also delivered a devastating blow to the idea and philosophy of secular pan-Arab nationalism. In six short days, Israel defeated the Arab nationalist states of Egypt, Syria, Iraq, and Jordan. These Arab states had been united in their commitment to the Arab people to fight for political independence, economic well-being through jobs and education, and self-determination for every Arab man, woman, and child, especially the dispersed Palestinian people. After the Six-Day War with Israel, all of these hopes and dreams were shattered. It was the second devastating defeat for the Palestinians in 20 years.

The war changed the balance of power not only between Israel and the surrounding Arab states, but also between the secular pan-Arab nationalists of Egypt and Syria, and the more conservative oil-exporting monarchies of the Arabian Peninsula. This created a regional political vacuum and gave guerrillas the opportunity to forge ahead with their own special method of waging political and military warfare. They became independent agents in the Palestinian, Arab, and Middle Eastern arenas. This would prove to be another crucial turning point in the Palestinian liberation struggle. Because the guerrillas seemed the only ones willing and able to forge ahead during this time of moral, spiritual, and political crisis, their revolutionary ideology became the new clarion call. It spread widely and deeply within the communities of the displaced Palestinians and throughout the Arab world.

But they were not to rule the day alone. The conservative Arab monarchies, which felt almost as threatened by the new Arab revolution as they did by Israel, also emerged from beneath the shadow of the defeated secular pan-Arab nationalism. As a result, two opposing factions emerged in the Middle East. One was revolutionary and led by the Palestinians. The other was conservative

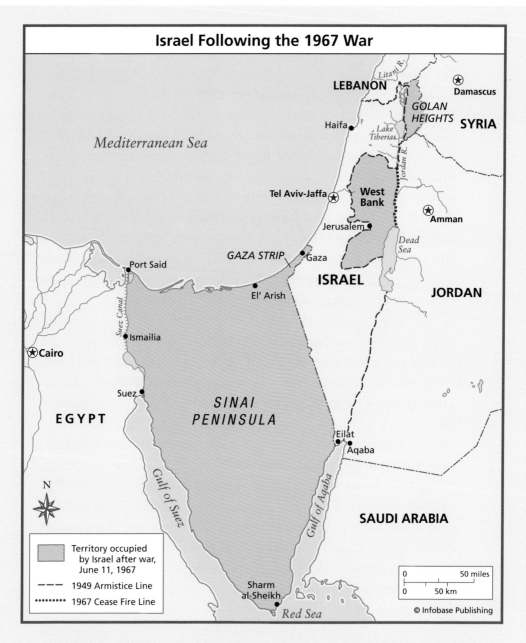

Israel Following the 1967 War

LEBANON
Damascus
GOLAN HEIGHTS
SYRIA
Litani R.
Haifa
Lake Tiberias
Mediterranean Sea
Jordan R.
Tel Aviv-Jaffa
West Bank
Amman
Jerusalem
Dead Sea
GAZA STRIP   Gaza
Port Said
ISRAEL
JORDAN
El' Arish
Suez Canal
Ismailia
Cairo
Suez
SINAI PENINSULA
Eilat
Aqaba
EGYPT
N
Gulf of Suez
Gulf of Aqaba
SAUDI ARABIA

Territory occupied by Israel after war, June 11, 1967
- - - 1949 Armistice Line
••••• 1967 Cease Fire Line

| 0 | 50 miles |
| 0 | 50 km |

Sharm al-Sheikh
Red Sea
© Infobase Publishing

The Six-Day War was an enormous victory for Israel, as they defeated several Arab opponents in the conflict, including Egypt, Syria, Iraq, and Jordan. Not only was this win demoralizing for the Palestinians, but the entire region felt a shift in power as Israel occupied territories in Egypt and Syria.

and led by Saudi Arabia and the defeated Arab nationalist state of Egypt, led by Gamal Abdel Nasser. Before the 1967 defeat, Nasser had represented the forefront of the liberation struggle. The conflict between these two opposing personalities, the revolutionary and the conservative, would define the boundaries of the Palestinian liberation struggle for the next four decades.

THE RISE OF ARAFAT

In March 1968, less than a year after the Six-Day War, the PLO guerrillas won fame by repelling an Israeli attack on PLO bases in Jordan. A year later, Yasir Arafat, the leader of Fatah, was elected chairman of the PLO. Later, in 1971, Arafat became commander in chief of the Palestinian Revolutionary Forces. Two years after that, he became head of the PLO's political department. From that point forward, he directed his efforts increasingly toward political persuasion rather than confrontation and terrorism against Israel.

Fatah, as most influential group of fedayeen, wasted little time in asserting itself. In March 1968, the Israeli army attacked PLO bases in Jordan. The Palestinian forces, under the command of Arafat, succeeded in fending off the Israelis. The following year, he was elected chairman of the PLO.

In the 1970s, a violent wing of Fatah, known as Black September, organized a series of devastating attacks. Black September's most notorious action came when gunmen kidnapped and assassinated 11 Israeli athletes in Munich, West Germany, during the 1972 Summer Olympics. This event (during which five Palestinians and a German police officer were also killed) drew international attention to the Palestinian cause, but its violence shocked the world.

"Do Not Let the Olive Branch Fall From My Hand"

Arafat continued to strengthen his power within the PLO. By 1973, he was head of its political department. In this role he

Although the guerrilla movement had largely influenced the PLO, Yasir Arafat *(above right)* used his position as president of the organization to attempt non-violent negotiations with Israel. Here, Arafat chats with Egyptian president Anwar Sadat, who signed a peace treaty with Israel in 1979.

emphasized political persuasion rather than terrorism, although his refusal to condemn terrorist activity made him, in the minds of many, still a terrorist. Nonetheless, his efforts at diplomacy continued and in 1974 the Arab nations recognized the PLO as the sole legitimate representative of the Palestinian people.

The same year, Arafat addressed a session of the United Nations General Assembly. During his speech, Arafat made a now-famous remark: "I have come bearing an olive branch and a freedom fighter's gun. Do not let the olive branch fall from my hand."

But diplomacy alone failed to change the nature of the conflict. In 1982, Israel destroyed PLO strongholds in Lebanon. An estimated 12,000 Palestinians fled, to several Arab countries.

Many Palestinians grew disillusioned by the failure of the PLO's diplomatic efforts. In 1987, in the Gaza Strip, a spontaneous revolt against Israel began. It was known as the *intifada*, which means "rebellion" or "shaking off."

It was an attempt to liberate portions of Palestine through a combination of force and negotiation. However, as the intifada continued, the violent aspects of the uprising dominated. The Israeli military responded with increased violence from its side.

In 1988, Arafat declared that the West Bank and Gaza were to be an independent Palestinian state. Furthermore, he declared, he was renouncing terrorism completely. He stated that everyone—including the Israelis—deserved to live in peace. Nonetheless, the intifada continued, into the next phase in the convoluted, complicated history of the Palestinians.

An Unclear and Troubled Independence

Arafat's official policy of favoring diplomacy over overt terrorism gradually won a measure of support for the cause of an independent Palestine. The PLO began carrying out secret peace talks with Israel. These culminated in 1993, when the PLO leader and the Israeli prime minister Yitzhak Rabin signed a landmark agreement. It was the first of a series of peace documents called the Oslo Accords. For this achievement, Arafat, Rabin, and Israeli Foreign Minister Shimon Peres shared the 1994 Nobel Peace Prize.

The Oslo talks led to the formal creation of the Palestinian Authority. The two sides also agreed to recognize each other diplomatically. Furthermore, they agreed to some (but not all) terms for the future of the West Bank and the Gaza Strip, both of which had overwhelmingly large Palestinian populations who felt the brunt of the conflict. According to the agreement, these regions would gradually be handed over to the Palestinian National Authority, which would assume control of such key civil functions as education, criminal justice, health care, and sanitation. Arafat easily won the election to become the first president of the new Palestinian National Authority, and voters elected a council to help him govern.

All of this represented a major step forward, but the Oslo Accords proved to be a mixed success. The agreement called for a complete handover of the disputed territories within five years. Still, the situation remained highly volatile and unsettled after the five-year deadline—a condition that persists to the present time and indeed, has become much worse.

THE AFTERMATH OF THE OSLO ACCORDS

Not all Palestinians approved of the Oslo Accords. Several militant Islamic groups bitterly denounced the agreement. The most prominent of these groups was Hamas, the largest of the militant Palestinian organizations. Hamas takes its name from the Arabic word for "zeal." The name also is short for *Harakat al-Muqawama al-Islamiyya*, or Islamic Resistance Movement. It was founded in 1987 as an outgrowth of the first intifada.

Hamas had two faces. It was largely focused on creating such organizations as charities, clinics, and schools for Palestinians within the occupied territories. On the other side, it also believed in armed resistance against the Israelis. It called for the destruction of Israel and the creation of an independent, Islamic Palestine through *jihad* ("struggle"). Hamas leaders considered the Oslo Accords a sellout because the agreements acknowledged Israel's right to exist. The accords also did not create a fully independent Palestinian state, and they left unanswered such hard issues as refugee status and the fate of the holy city of Jerusalem.

Some Jewish factions also strongly opposed the Oslo Accords. These hard-liners in Israel remained unwilling to compromise with the Palestinians. Opposition to the peace process within Israel reached a dramatic climax in November 1995, when Yitzhak Rabin, one of the key figures in the Oslo Accords, was assassinated. The killer was a Jewish religious fanatic who had hoped to stop the peace process. Instead, Rabin's death caused a surge in Jewish popular support for peace, at least in the short term. Shimon Peres, Rabin's successor as prime minister (and also a key figure in the Oslo Accords), was able to move ahead with the process until he was defeated by Benjamin Netanyahu in the 1996 election.

DISAPPOINTMENT

Despite high hopes, the promises of the Oslo Accords proved to be deep disappointments for many Jews and Arabs alike. Both sides blamed the other for defying the spirit of the peace agreements in the following years.

Islamic fighters, primarily organized by Hamas and another radical group, Islamic Jihad, continued to wage guerrilla warfare against Israel. In particular, they staged devastating suicide bombing missions in Jerusalem, Tel Aviv, and other Israeli cities. Arafat was severely criticized, both by Israel and by its supporters abroad, for allowing these terrorists to train and carry out their violent acts. Furthermore, critics charged, the Palestinian National Authority's official armed service, though meant to be an internal police force, was in effect a paramilitary force. This was a violation of the Oslo Accords.

Meanwhile, Israel insisted on its right to defend itself and to launch its own attacks. In a move that was directly in opposition to the accords, the Israeli government allowed the number of Jewish settlements in the West Bank to grow. They doubled in the seven years after the Oslo signing, from housing about 220,000 settlers in 1993 to 450,000 settlers by 2000.

The Palestinians won some significant advantages from the Oslo Accords, but they still suffered serious obstacles. Palestinians who worked in Jewish areas still were highly restricted in their movements, and they had to endure a net increase in Israeli settlement in their own territories. Palestinians also were still isolated from the important religious center of Jerusalem.

Furthermore, the vast majority of Palestinians still lived in dire poverty because their economy was in deep decline.

This was due in large part to a shift in the Israeli job market. Many Israeli businesses began using foreign workers instead of Palestinians. This saved money and solved some security issues for the Israelis, but it impoverished many Palestinians. It has been estimated that as much as 60 percent of the population in the Gaza Strip lived below the poverty line during the 1990s.

Despite the continuing presence of such serious problems, the peace process slowly moved forward. By early 1996, nearly all Palestinians in the West Bank and Gaza were under self-rule, although Israeli military forces still were present in these disputed areas.

CAMP DAVID

Another significant step in the peace process occurred in 2000, when U.S. President Bill Clinton helped organize another Middle East summit at Camp David, Maryland. At this meeting, then–Israeli Prime Minister Ehud Barak outlined a plan that would have given the Palestinians several significant concessions, including:

- ♦ Control of some 90 percent of the West Bank and all of the Gaza Strip
- ♦ The establishment of a Palestinian capital in East Jerusalem, where several Arab neighborhoods would become Palestinian territory
- ♦ Palestinian rule over half of the Old City of Jerusalem
- ♦ Partial custodianship of the Al-Aqsa Mosque (also known as the Temple Mount), a site holy to Muslims, Jews, and Christians alike
- ♦ Conditional return of refugees to the Palestinian state

These were all significant concessions, and yet Arafat rejected Barak's plan. The Israeli media severely criticized him for doing so. Arafat insisted that the plan be amended to include several other points. Among these were that Israel give up all control of the holy site of the Western Wall (also called the Wailing Wall) in the Temple Mount. As a result of this disagreement, the Camp David talks collapsed and a new uprising, a second intifada, began.

Organized by U.S. President Clinton *(far left)* in 2000, the Camp David meeting between PLO leader Yasir Arafat and Israeli Prime Minister Ehud Barak *(above, right)* broke down when neither representative stood firm on their demands. This breakdown in negotiations proved deadly, as a second intifada began in the Middle East.

THE SECOND INTIFADA BEGINS

This new round of violence had been brewing for some time, but one incident in particular helped touch it off: a highly publicized and controversial visit in September 2000 by Ariel Sharon (at that point the opposition leader in the Israeli government) to the Al-Aqsa Mosque. Sharon's visit outraged Palestinians, who saw it as an insensitive attempt to assert Israeli authority over the site.

The second intifada, sometimes called the Al-Aqsa intifada, was much bloodier than the first. Its thrust was a massive wave of suicide bombings. When Arafat proved unable or unwilling to control the violence, Israel attacked Arafat's police forces, destroyed his helicopters, and isolated the PLO leader in his headquarters in the West Bank city of Ramallah. Israeli tanks also invaded several West Bank cities.

As always during this period, the fate of the Palestinians was directly tied to Israeli politics. In 2001, Ariel Sharon won a landslide victory to become the country's next prime minister, and he remained in office for a second term. Sharon's focus was on greater security for his country, including construction of a massive wall between most of the West Bank and Israel. It did not exactly follow the pre-1967 border, and it created many hardships for the Palestinians. (In July 2004, the International Court of Justice ruled that this barrier violated international law and had to be torn down. It has not been dismantled, despite this ruling, but some changes were made.)

The violence, as well as attempts to restart the peace process, continued sporadically. In particular, guerrilla activity in Gaza increased. In 2002, Israel announced a policy of seizing Palestinian-held land in the West Bank in retaliation for the terrorist attacks.

In spring 2003, the so-called Quartet (the United States, the European Union, the UN, and the Russian Federation) presented to Israel and to the Palestinian Authority a new peace proposal, dubbed a "roadmap for peace." It called for Palestinian leadership that could support decisive action against terrorism and toward democracy. It also called for an end to Israeli occupation of the disputed territories by 2005.

ENTER ABBAS

Meanwhile, Yasser Arafat's hold on Palestinian politics was growing weaker. The Israeli military continued to confine him in a virtual house arrest at his headquarters in Ramallah. This isolation caused the Palestinian leader to become increasingly irrelevant, politically speaking. His failing health and rumors of corruption in his government also served to marginalize him in his last years.

Israel and the United States viewed Arafat with disdain, declaring that they had lost faith in him as someone they could count on. They regarded him as still too closely linked to terrorism, despite his denials of that, and they felt that he was unwilling or unable to stop the ongoing violence. Both Israel and the United States therefore refused to negotiate with him any longer. Instead, they aided factions within the Palestinian National Authority that hoped to minimize his influence.

To this end, the new post of prime minister was established within the Palestinian National Authority in 2003. The moderate Mahmoud Abbas was the first person to hold this position. Abbas's family members had been refugees in Syria after the 1948 Arab-Israeli war, and he himself was a lawyer and one of the founders of Fatah. He also headed the PLO's international department in the late 1970s and had played a key role in the peace negotiations in the following decades.

Abbas's elevation to the post of prime minister helped to circumvent Arafat's influence. It put someone who favored diplomacy into a position of power over someone who favored violent action. Abbas rejected terrorism, supported an end to the intifada, and promised to create a single, unified, and controllable Palestinian armed forces. Furthermore, he was someone with whom the opposition felt it could negotiate in good faith.

THE END OF AN ERA

Despite Abbas's presence, Yasir Arafat wielded enough clout to engineer the new prime minister's resignation soon after his appointment. Abbas stated at the time that he was stepping down because Arafat's refusal to share power made his position impossible. Ahmed Qurei, another veteran Palestinian politician, succeeded him.

Although he remained isolated in Ramallah, Arafat continued to cling to power until he became gravely ill in late 2004. Near death, Arafat was flown to France for medical treatment. He died in Paris in November 2004 at the age of 75. The exact cause is unknown. Reports that he was poisoned, or that he had AIDS or an unusual liver or blood disease, have remained just speculation. His wife refused to allow an autopsy, which would probably have answered the question. Following a funeral service in Cairo, Egypt, Arafat's body was returned to Ramallah, where thousands of mourners gathered for the burial.

Yasir Arafat's death marked the end of an era for Palestinians. For nearly 40 years, his name had been synonymous with the cause of the stateless Palestinian people. Under his leadership, the PLO had gained power and international prestige. He had done much to create a movement dedicated to the idea that Palestinian Arabs had the right to a country of their own.

Arafat also was severely criticized during his lifetime and after. He was denounced for his dictatorial ways. He was criticized for allowing widespread corruption and inefficiency that, in turn, did little to improve the dire standard of living for Palestinians. Most of all, he was condemned for his ongoing support—unspoken or not—of violent terrorism.

MORE VIOLENCE

As Arafat was living out his last days, diplomats for the Quartet were working to put their "roadmap for peace" into play. The set deadline of 2005 proved to be overly optimistic. The two sides had come no closer to a permanent peace, and the violence of the second intifada continued. Events such as the assassinations in 2004 by Israeli troops of Ahmed Yassin, the founder and leader of Hamas, and of his successor, Abdel Aziz al-Rantisi, did nothing to stop the bloodshed. Israel's wall and the growth of Jewish settlements also derailed the process.

In July 2004, in response to the Palestinian National Authority's failure to carry out its promised reforms, Palestine faced the blocking of international aid. U.S. President George W. Bush, who had always firmly backed Israel, expressed doubt about the immediate future's prospects for peace between the Palestinians and Israelis because of the Palestinian National Authority's instability and the continuing violence.

Meanwhile, rival factions among the Palestinians were clashing more often and more violently. In 2004, for example, the mayor of Nablus resigned in order to protest the Palestinian National Authority's refusal to curb armed militias in his city, and also because there had been several attempts to assassinate him—not by Israelis but by Palestinians. That same year, attacks on a number of Palestinian journalists were widely blamed on rival Palestinian factions.

The violence sometimes spilled over to affect groups that were neither Jewish nor Palestinian. In October 2003, for example, three members of a U.S. diplomatic convoy were killed, and additional members of the convoy were wounded, by a bomb in the Gaza Strip. Those responsible for this attack were never identified or captured.

THE SECOND INTIFADA WANES

Even after he had officially renounced terrorism, Arafat was widely blamed for allowing attacks to continue. Some observers feared that his death would create a power struggle and a marked increase in violence. Instead, the transition of power within the Palestinian Authority was remarkably smooth and peaceful.

Mahmoud Abbas, the former prime minister, succeeded Arafat as chairman of the PLO. Early in 2005, he won the election for the leadership of the Palestinian National Authority. It was a landslide victory: Abbas garnered 62.3 percent of the vote while his closest rival, independent candidate Dr. Mustafa Barghouti, won only 19.8 percent.

Meanwhile, the violence began to wane. One reason for this was that Abbas, bowing to international pressure and threats of retaliation from Israel, ordered hundreds of Palestinian police into the northern part of the Gaza Strip. They were instructed to prevent further violence, including rocket and mortar shelling of Israeli settlements.

Another development came early in 2005, when Abbas and Sharon signed a truce agreement at a meeting called the Sharm el-Sheikh Summit. (It was named for the Egyptian resort where the meeting took place.) Hamas and Islamic Jihad—which remained staunchly in favor of armed rebellion—bitterly denounced the truce and said that it did not apply to them. These groups continued their attacks on Israeli settlements.

A NEW PLAN

Also in 2005, a third factor emerged that helped stem the ongoing violence. This was a surprising turn of events on the Israeli side: a serious plan to withdraw all Israeli troops and settlers from the Gaza Strip.

Ariel Sharon, the father of the Israeli settlement movement, left his longtime political party, the Likud, and formed a new party called Kadima ("Forward"). This party was created with the express purpose of putting forward a peace plan that would include significant concessions to the Palestinians. Sharon did not, however, go as far with his proposal as Barak had gone during the 2000 Camp David talks. Nonetheless, Sharon's plan proposed, among other things, a withdrawal of Israeli troops and settlers from the Gaza Strip and from four neighborhoods in the West Bank.

Sharon clearly stated that the occupation of Gaza had become more of a liability than an asset to Israel. His goal was to create

A historic summit between Palestinian leader Mahmoud Abbas *(right)* and Israeli Prime Minister Ariel Sharon *(left)* in 2005 helped quiet violent incidents in the Middle East. In these talks, the Israeli government pledged to withdraw from the Gaza Strip, one of the most fought-over areas of the world.

an Israel made up of mostly Jews, living inside a secure border. This version of Israel would include the land it already had before the June 1967 war, plus about 8 percent of the West Bank and most of East Jerusalem.

The Palestinian people have always wanted East Jerusalem as the site of their future capital. Many Palestinians therefore strongly denounced Sharon's proposal as not going far enough. A number of hard-line Israelis, both politicians and citizens, also opposed the proposal, but for the opposite reason. Despite such opposition, in August 2005, Sharon began to put his plan into action.

ISRAEL WITHDRAWS FROM GAZA

The Gaza Strip is small, poor, and arid. Most of its 1.5 million inhabitants are Palestinian refugees or their descendants. Those who live there have fewer job opportunities and are even more constrained by Israeli and Egyptian security than those who live in the West Bank. Nonetheless, Gaza has long been one of the most bitterly contested regions in the world, and Israel's withdrawal from it had profound implications for peace throughout the Middle East.

For nearly 4 decades before the withdrawal in 2005, Israelis had occupied 21 settlements in Gaza. Most of these Jewish settlers left peacefully when the withdrawal orders came through, although some protested, and Israeli troops had to forcibly remove them. There were no major incidents of violence on either side, though, and Israel was completely out of the Gaza Strip and four areas in the West Bank by the end of August 2005.

Still, there were points of contention between the Israelis and the Palestinians. Notably, Israel was continuing to build its controversial security barrier along the West Bank border. Israel also was encouraging the new construction of Jewish settlements in certain areas of the West Bank. Many observers saw these actions as part of a plan to ensure that an ultra-secure, all-Jewish state would, in the future, include most of the West Bank.

A TENTATIVE END TO THE INTIFADA

Thanks to several factors—notably the rejuvenated efforts at diplomacy on the part of Mahmoud Abbas, and the Sharon-led withdrawal from the West Bank—violence in the disputed territories continued to die down significantly throughout 2005. The intifada never officially ended, but the level of fighting dropped so dramatically that many observers felt it had essentially ended.

All told, it has been estimated that some 1,000 Israelis and 3,500 Palestinians died during the worst of the second intifada, from 2000 to 2005. These estimates include both military personnel and civilians. In addition, tens of thousands more on both sides were wounded, some seriously. Still, as the year ended, many had hopes that a real breakthrough in the Palestine issue was imminent.

The year 2006, however, proved to be extremely chaotic. The uncertainty began in January, when Ariel Sharon, who had done much to stimulate and sustain the peace process, suffered a massive stroke and was unable to continue in office. Sharon was replaced by Ehud Olmert, an acting prime minister. Olmert formed a coalition government that included several widely varied Israeli political groups, from hard-liners to the concession-minded.

A SURPRISE VICTORY FOR HAMAS

During the same period, the Palestinian National Authority held its own legislative elections, the first such election in a decade. Fatah—the party of Arafat and Abbas, and the dominant force in Palestinian politics for more than four decades—was expected by Israel and by most foreign commentators to win a clear majority.

The Hamas party instead scored a surprise victory. It won 76 seats out of 132 in the newly expanded Palestinian Legislative Council. An additional 4 seats went to candidates who were sympathetic to Hamas. Fatah won only 43 seats, and the rest went to smaller parties or independents. Hamas thus gained control of the Palestinian National Authority for the first time. Abbas remained the president, and Hamas leader Ismail Haniyeh became prime minister.

Voters apparently saw the Hamas party as offering fresh leadership. The hope was that it might prove more effective than Fatah had been at establishing a homeland for the Palestinians. The voters also hoped that Hamas could avoid the corruption and ineffectiveness that had plagued Fatah. Voters also seemed to see Hamas as offering the hope of decisive action against Israel. Haniyeh, a hard-liner, openly defied the aspirations of Abbas. The new prime minister stated that the Palestinian National

Authority would never acknowledge the legitimacy of a Jewish state. "We will never recognize the usurper Zionist government," he declared, "and will continue our *jihad*-like movement until the liberation of Jerusalem."

SANCTIONS

Clearly, there was strong potential for tension between Hamas and Fatah, which share many of the same goals but also differ sharply in many ways. Nonetheless, the two parties were able to form a shaky coalition government.

Meanwhile, militant Palestinians continued to attack Israel across the borders. Israel retaliated by sending troops back into the Gaza Strip in the summer of 2006. During this time, Israel also bombed and temporarily occupied parts of Lebanon. Anti-Israeli forces, notably Hezbollah troops, were stationed there and had two Israeli soldiers held hostage.

Internationally, Hamas's electoral victory was widely criticized or regarded with skepticism. Ehud Olmert, who became Israel's prime minister in April 2006, has said that he regards any Hamas-led government of the Palestinian National Authority as hostile, and that he will not negotiate with Hamas unless it disarms. The United States and the European Union, two other influential international parties in the issue, officially consider Hamas a terrorist organization. After Hamas's victory, therefore, strict economic sanctions were brought against the Palestinian National Authority by a number of countries.

The UN warned, correctly, that the severe cuts in funding as a result of sanctions would result in a humanitarian crisis for the Palestinians. Because of the sanctions, the Palestinian economy struggled to stay afloat because the money it desperately needed was not available. The problems created by such sanctions only added to the existing severe poverty, unemployment, and homelessness already suffered by Palestinians in the disputed territories.

Hamas hoped that funds from various Arab countries and other Muslim states would replace this lost Western aid. The replacement money was not enough, though, and the Palestinian economy had almost completely collapsed by the end of 2006. President Abbas—who still enjoys wide support in the West and whom Israel considers a good negotiating partner—was forced to dissolve his government.

THE GAZA WAR

Meanwhile, infighting between the two main factions of the Palestinian National Authority continued. In June 2007, this culminated in a series of bloody clashes between Hamas and Fatah security forces in the Gaza Strip. Commonly known as the Gaza War, this violence ended with Hamas taking effective control of the Gaza Strip. The West Bank remains under effective control of Fatah.

Since the Gaza War, the region has been almost completely sealed off, politically and economically. Its border crossings have been closed to the transfer of all but essential goods. Since businesses inside Gaza cannot export anything, the economy has plummeted. According to a UN survey, only about 10 percent of Gaza's industries are doing any productive work. Millions of dollars worth of potential business has been lost, and since little comes in, the condition of the populace there has grown steadily worse.

The Gaza War threw an already volatile situation into even greater flux. President Abbas declared a state of emergency and dismissed Prime Minister Haniyeh. Abbas replaced him with former Finance Minister Salam Fayyad. Fayyad is a moderate who, like Abbas, favors recognizing Israel. Together they head the government that effectively controls the West Bank.

Several countries and organizations, including Israel, the United States, and the European Union, have responded favorably to this change in leadership, away from the radical Hamas. They have indicated a willingness to resume providing financial aid and other help to a Palestinian government that does not include Hamas. In 2007, the United States, European countries, and Israel pledged hundreds of millions of dollars of support for a Fatah-led government.

Many observers fear that Fatah will, in the end, prove ineffective. Abbas had hoped to replace the PLO's militant image with one that favored diplomacy and conciliation. Fatah, however, has a long way to go to shake its legacy of financial corruption, abuse of power, mismanagement, and weak leadership. What that means for the Palestinian National Authority in the long run is still hard to predict.

TONY BLAIR ENTERS THE FRAY

The month after the Gaza War took place, in July 2007, still another factor entered the ongoing situation. Tony Blair, who had just stepped down as the prime minister of the United Kingdom, was appointed special envoy of the Quartet consisting of the European Union, the United States, the UN, and Russia.

Blair began his new job with a round of talks. He met with the foreign ministers of Jordan and Israel, President Abbas and Prime Minister Fayyad, and others. He did not, however, speak with representatives of Hamas, despite a warning from Hamas leaders that attempts to ignore their organization would hurt Blair's credibility and his chances of success.

The new envoy's primary task was to help build the Palestinian National Authority's weak infrastructure and to stimulate its troubled economy. Some observers have expressed doubt, though, that Blair—who is in many ways a skilled negotiator and politician—can be effective. His predecessor, former World Bank president James D. Wolfensohn, lasted less than a year before he resigned in frustration. Wolfensohn blamed the Palestinians and the Israelis, as well as the United States, for hampering his efforts. Some feel that Blair will experience the same difficulties. Palestinian policy analyst Ghassan Khatib flatly states, "Appointing an envoy means nothing."

TIME FOR THE POLITICAL STAGE

Of course, with or without the help of an outside envoy, the relationship between Israel and the Palestinian National Authority remains at the heart of this ongoing conflict. As of mid-2007, the incumbent Israeli prime minister, Ehud Olmert, has said that he is not ready to discuss the toughest issues—primarily border disputes, the future of Jerusalem, and the fate of Palestinian refugees. He accurately reflects the mood of many, if not most, Israeli voters. Meanwhile, the Palestinians remain deeply split, with moderate Fatah effectively governing the West Bank, and the more radical Hamas effectively controlling the Gaza Strip.

The possibility for nonviolent reconciliation still remains open. As of mid-2007, the extremist group Islamic Jihad remains committed to violent resistance against Israel and has taken responsibility for ongoing suicide bombings and other attacks there. In the West Bank, however, Fatah has been working to maintain a ceasefire. The push to end the violence there may be taking hold. A number of former militants connected with Fatah have heeded President Abbas's plea to end the violence and to embrace diplomacy. These militants handed in their weapons and signed pledges promising to cease violence against Israel.

Among these former militants were members of the Aqsa Martyrs' Brigades, an especially aggressive group within Fatah's military wing that played a key role in the second intifada. They have stated that they are willing to give Abbas a chance to consolidate his rule and to concentrate on political diplomacy. "Everything must come to an end," said Mahdi Maraka, a leader within the Aqsa Martyrs' Brigades. "There are two tracks, the political and the military. Now is the time for the political stage."

MORE SIGNS OF RECONCILIATION, MORE UNANSWERED QUESTIONS

Israel also has been indicating that it is open to reconciliation. The Israeli government announced that it will offer immunity to many of the most notorious Palestinian terrorists. Meanwhile, Israel has released some 250 Palestinian prisoners and also plans to remove some of the internal checkpoints in the West Bank that continue to be especially troublesome to Palestinians. Furthermore, the possibility holds out that the

Because of shifting regional politics and the emergence of new military groups like Hamas *(above)*, the future of Palestine remains unclear. Continued diplomatic relations with Israel and other countries and trust in their own leadership remain pivotal to Palestine's development and survival.

remaining Jewish settlers in the occupied territories—an estimated 187,000 in the West Bank and somewhat fewer than 177,000 in East Jerusalem—will someday leave.

For both sides, the tentative slowing of the violence is just an experiment. Most doubt the chances for success of any permanent peace. Mahdi Abdul Hadi, the director of the Palestinian research institute Passia, states, "In Palestinian history there are no beginnings and no ends. There are unfolding chapters, like waves in the sea."

The future remains uncertain. Who will lead the Palestinian National Authority into the future? Will the radical factions within it change their militant stance, or will they continue to say that Israel's destruction is the only answer? Will the more moderate factions prevail, insisting that nonviolent diplomacy holds the key? Meanwhile, who will dominate in Israel: hard-liners, or moderates willing to make concessions to the Palestinians?

"JEWS AND ARABS ARE FATALLY ALIKE"

The quickly shifting events, the bitterly fought battles, the changing degree of effectiveness of political leaders, and many more factors indicate that the future of peace—and Palestinian statehood—will remain in question for some time to come. In large part, this is because it is sometimes forgotten, when discussing the current state of ancient feuds, that the feuds are fought by groups and that groups are made up of individuals. Too often, when discussing Arabs and Jews, the traits of individual humans are forgotten.

Both groups are made up of regular human beings who are, in some ways, remarkably similar. At the same time, both groups also have important grievances that should not be minimized. Journalist Tim McGirk, reporting in *Time* magazine on a conversation with an ordinary Palestinian named Omar, commented:

I ask him if Jews and Palestinians are so different. No, he says. They're both smart, they value education, and they laugh at the same jokes. But in conversation with Omar, I realize that Jews and Arabs are fatally alike in another way: They both suffer from a powerful and justifiable sense of victimization—the Jews over the Holocaust, the Palestinians over the loss of their land—and this blinds them to the others' tragedy.

A NEW GENERATION

The future of the Palestinian National Authority, of course, depends on its next generations. Statistically, the Palestinian people are overwhelmingly youthful: According to the Palestinian Central Bureau of Statistics, more than half of all Palestinians are under 19, and more than three-quarters of the population in the Gaza Strip is under 30.

Some young Palestinians, having grown up knowing little more than war and poverty, despair of ever having a state of their own. Still, many in the current generation of young Palestinians continue to hope for a Palestinian state—and unfortunately, many of them think that armed struggle is the way to achieve it. Recent opinion polls conducted by the Palestinian Center for Policy and Survey Research indicate that young Palestinians, as a whole, are more supportive of violent terrorism than their parents. More than half of those under 30 expect more violent struggles with Israel in the next 5 to 10 years. Only about one-fifth think a peaceful solution is possible, and nearly half think that such an agreement is impossible.

The violent tendencies of young Palestinians are directed toward Israel, of course, but often also toward one another. The pressure to identify oneself with one Palestinian faction or another can be strong. A university student named Shadi el-Haj commented to the *New York Times*:

> We're pushed all the time to be more political, more militant, more religious, more extreme. We want to be Palestinians, like the generation of the first *intifada*. But people push you, 'Are

you Fatah or Hamas?' All our problems start with, 'I'm Fatah, I'm Hamas.' It wasn't like that before.

The power struggle between these two factions, vying for control of the future of Palestine, will no doubt play a major role in determining the fate of the Palestinian people as a whole.

Chronology

B.C.

3000–2000   Arrival and settlement of the Canaanites in Palestine.

1250   Approximate date of Israelite conquest of Canaan.

1000–962   Reign of King David.

965–928   King Solomon's construction of the Temple of Jerusalem.

928   Division of the Israelites into the kingdoms of Israel and Judah.

721   Assyrian conquest of Israel.

586   Judah defeated by Babylonians under King Nebuchadnezzar; deportation of Jews into Babylon and destruction of the temple.

539   Persia conquers Babylon, allows Jews to return to Israel; construction of new temple.

334–333   Alexander the Great conquers Persia; Palestine comes under Macedonian rule.

323   Alexander the Great dies; Ptolemies of Egypt followed by Seleucids of Syria rule Palestine.

167   Maccabees revolt against the Seleucid ruler and establish independent state.

63   Palestine becomes part of the Roman Empire.

A.D.

70   Destruction of Second Temple by Roman Emperor Titus.

132–135   Suppression of Bar Kokhba Revolt; Jews barred from Jerusalem and Emperor Hadrian builds a pagan city on its ruins.

330–638   Palestine ruled by Byzantine Empire; Christianity spreads in this region.

638 Omar ibn al-Khattab enters Jerusalem and ends Byzantine rule.

661–750 Palestine becomes a province under the Arab-Islamic Umayyad dynasty that was based in Damascus.

685–691 The Umayyad caliph Abdul Malik Ibn Marwan (685–705) builds the Dome of the Rock in Jerusalem.

705 al-Walid Ibn Abdul Malik (705–715) of the Umayyads builds al-Aqsa Mosque in Jerusalem.

750–1258 Palestine becomes a province of the Abbasid dynasty in Baghdad.

Timeline

1000–962 B.C.
Reign of King David

685–691
Abdul Malik Ibn Marwan builds the Dome of the Rock in Jerusalem

1099–1187
Crusaders invade Palestine and establish the Latin kingdom of Jerusalem

1517–1918
Palestine under Ottoman rule

1917
Balfour Declaration supports Jewish national home in Palestine

1000 B.C.   1918

63 B.C.
Palestine becomes part of the Roman Empire

330–638 A.D.
Palestine ruled by Byzantine Empire; Christianity spreads

1897
First Zionist congress meets in Basel, Switzerland

1915–1916
Hussein-McMahon Correspondence guarantees Arab independence and new Arab nation

1099–1187	The Crusaders invade Palestine and establish the Latin kingdom of Jerusalem.
1187	The Battle of Hittin in Palestine; Saladin of Egypt defeats the Crusaders and liberates Palestine from European control.
1517	Ottoman conquest of most of the Arab world, including Palestine.
1517–1918	Palestine under Ottoman rule.
1882–1904	First wave of immigration of Jewish settlers to Palestine.
1897	First Zionist congress meets in Basel, Switzerland.

1948
Zionists declare the independent state of Israel

2000
Camp David negotiations fail; Ariel Sharon visits the Temple Mount, setting off violent clashes

1967
Six-Day War; Israel gains Sinai Peninsula, Gaza Strip, West Bank, and Golan Heights and reunites Jerusalem

1948   **2005**

1957
Yasir Arafat helps found the Palestine Liberation Movement, whose name becomes Fatah

1987
First intifada begins in Gaza and spreads to the West Bank

1993
PLO establishes the PA and appoints Arafat as its head; Rabin and Arafat sign Declaration of Principles

2005
Mahmoud Abbas takes office as president of the PNA after Arafat dies in 2004

1904–1914	Second wave of immigration of Jewish settlers to Palestine.
1911	*Filistine* newspaper founded in Jaffa by Issa al-Issa
1914	World War I starts.
1915–1916	Sharif Hussein and Henry McMahon exchange correspondence guaranteeing Arab independence.
1916	On May 16, Great Britain and France sign Sykes-Picot Agreement, which divides the Ottoman Middle East provinces among them.
1917	British Foreign Secretary Lord Arthur Balfour sends a letter (later known as the Balfour Declaration) to Lord Edmund de Rothschild, supporting the establishment of a Jewish national home in Palestine.
1918	British forces, led by General Allenby, occupy Palestine; Ottoman-British fighting ends in October, and World War I ends November 11.
1919	First National Conference-Palestine; King-Crane Commission established.
1920	San Remo Conference grants Great Britain a mandate over Palestine on April 24.
1922	Council of the League of Nations Mandate for Palestine on July 24; Churchill memorandum defines Great Britain's understanding of mandate.
1936–1939	Arab Revolt erupts in Palestine.
1937	The Peel Commission report recommends the partition of Palestine.
1939	The British government issues MacDonald White Paper restricting Jewish immigration.
1942	Biltmore Hotel Conference on May 11.
1946–1948	Jewish-Palestinian-British War.
1948	Al-Nakbah, or catastrophic destruction of Palestine, and the beginning of the Palestinian diaspora; Zionists declare the independent state of Israel.

1949 At the end of the War of 1948, Israel extends its holdings of Palestine.

1950 The West Bank becomes part of Jordan.

1953 Israel launches a large-scale assault on the Gaza Strip.

1956 Suez War.

1957 Yasir Arafat helps found the Palestine Liberation Movement, whose name becomes Fatah.

1964 The Palestine Liberation Organization is founded.

1967 Six-Day War.

1968 Battle of al-Karameh, in which Palestinian guerrillas prevent Israel from invading lands east of the Jordan River.

1974 Arab states recognize PLO as sole speaker for the Palestinian people.

1978 Israeli army invades Lebanon, demolishes villages, kills hundreds of Lebanese and Palestinians, and then withdraws.

1982 Israeli army invades Lebanon to destroy the military, political, and institutional infrastructure of the PLO; massacre at Sabra and Shatila facilitated by Israel.

1987 Palestinian intifada begins in Gaza and spreads to the West Bank.

1990 Saddam Hussein invades Kuwait, supported by the PLO.

1991 The United States and its allies attack Iraq, forcing Iraq to withdraw from Kuwait in the Gulf War; Yasir Arafat supports Iraq, and Palestinians are later expelled from Kuwait.

1993 PLO establishes the Palestinian National Authority and appoints Arafat as its head; Rabin and Arafat sign Declaration of Principles in Washington, D.C.; Oslo Accords.

1994 Palestinian National Authority holds its first meeting in Gaza City; Arafat, Rabin, and Peres accept the Nobel Peace Prize.

1996 Palestinian elections; Palestinian Legislative Council founded; Yasir Arafat elected president of the Palestinian National Authority.

1997 Palestinian National Authority and Israel sign protocol concerning the redeployment in Hebron (Hebron Agreement).

1998 Palestinian National Authority and Israel sign the Wye River Memorandum.

1999 King Hussein of Jordan dies; Palestine and Israel sign the Sharm el-Sheikh Memorandum (known as Wye II).

2000 Palestinian-Israeli negotiations at Camp David begin July 11 and later fail; Ariel Sharon visits the Temple Mount in Jerusalem, igniting a series of violent clashes known as al-Aqsa Intifada.

2001 Sharon is elected prime minister of Israel.

2002 More failed talks; Palestine and Israel engage in more violent confrontations.

2004 Yasir Arafat dies on November 11.

2005 Mahmoud Abbas takes office in January as president of the Palestinian National Authority.

Bibliography

Farsoun, Samih K. and Naseer H. Aruri. *Palestine and the Palestinians: A Social and Political History.* Boulder, Colo.: Westview Press, 2006.

Gerner, Deborah J. *One Land, Two Peoples: The Conflict Over Palestine.* Boulder, Colo.: Westview Press, 1991.

Hadawi, Sami. *Bitter Harvest: A Modern History of Palestine.* New York, N.Y.: Olive Branch Press, 1990.

Harms, Gregory. *The Palestine-Israel Conflict: A Basic Introduction.* Ann Arbor, Mich.: Pluto Press, 2005.

McGirk, Tim. "In the Shadow of 1967." *Time,* June 11, 2007.

Said, Edward W. *The Question of Palestine.* New York, N.Y.: Vintage Books, 1992.

Smith, Charles D. *Palestine and the Arab-Israeli Conflict A History with Documents.* 6th ed. New York, N.Y.: St. Martin's Press, 2006.

Tessler, Mark. *A History of the Israeli-Palestinian Conflict.* Bloomington, Ind.: Indiana University Press, 1994.

Further Resources

Bunton, Martin. *Colonial Land Policies in Palestine 1917–1936.*
New York, N.Y.: Oxford University Press, 2007.

Khalidi, Rashid. *The Iron Cage: The Story of the Palestinian Struggle
for Statehood.* Boston, Mass.: Beacon Press, 2006.

Kimmerling, Baruch and Joel S. Migdal. *The Palestinian People:
A History.* Cambridge, Mass.: Harvard University Press, 2003.

Laqueur, Walter and Barry Rubin, eds. *The Israel-Arab Reader:
A Documentary History of the Middle East Conflict.* 6th ed.
New York,N.Y.: Penguin Books, 2001.

Mattar, Philip. *Encyclopedia of the Palestinians.* New York, N.Y.:
Facts on File, 2005.

Mattar, Philip. *The Mufti of Jerusalem: Al-Hajj Amin al-Husayni and
the Palestinian National Movement.* New York, N.Y.: Columbia
University Press, 1988.

Pappe, Ilan. *A History of Modern Palestine: One Land, Two Peoples.*
New York, N.Y.: Cambridge University Press, 2004.

Segev, Tom. *One Palestine, Complete: Jews and Arabs Under the British
Mandate.* New York, N.Y.: Henry Holt, 1999.

Picture Credits

Index

About the Contributors

John G. Hall received a bachelor's degree in African-American Studies and American Literature from the University of Massachusetts in Boston and a master's degree in education from Converse College in Spartanburg, South Carolina. He has contributed fiction, nonfiction, and poetry to *African Voices, Aim Magazine, BackHome, Black Diaspora, Listen Magazine,* and *The Sounds of Poetry.* Hall and his wife live with their daughter in the mountains of western North Carolina.

Adam Woog has written about 60 books for adults, young adults, and children. He has a special interest in biography and history. He also writes a monthly column on crime and mystery fiction for the *Seattle Times.* Woog lives with his wife and daughter in his hometown of Seattle, Washington.

Series editor **Arthur Goldschmidt Jr.** is a retired professor of Middle East History at Penn State University. He has a B.A. in economics from Colby College and his M.A. and Ph.D. degrees from Harvard University in History and Middle Eastern Studies. He is the author of *A Concise History of the Middle East*, which has gone through eight editions, and many books, chapters, and articles about Egypt and other Middle Eastern countries. His most recent publication is *A Brief History of Egypt*, published by Facts On File in 2008. He lives in State College, Pennsylvania, with his wife, Louise. They have two grown sons.